SUBVERSIVE

CHRIST, CULTURE, AND THE SHOCKING

DOROTHY L. SAYERS

SUBVERSIVE

CHRIST, CULTURE, AND THE SHOCKING
DOROTHY L. SAYERS

CRYSTAL L. DOWNING

 Broadleaf Books

Minneapolis

SUBVERSIVE
Christ, Culture, and the Shocking
Dorothy L. Sayers

All Bible quotations are from the New Revised Standard Version, unless otherwise noted.

Permission to quote the works of Dorothy L. Sayers has been granted by David Higham and Associates Limited.

Cover design and illustration: James Kegley

Print ISBN: 978-1-5064-6275-2
eBook ISBN: 978-1-5064-6276-9

This book is dedicated to Christopher Dean (1932–2012), Chairman of the Dorothy L. Sayers Society from 1994 to 2012, who inspired me, as he did many others, with his passionate intellect and gracious encouragement

TABLE OF CONTENTS

Acknowledgments
ix

INTRODUCTION
The Murder of God
1

CHAPTER ONE
The Shock of the New
17

CHAPTER TWO
Religious Shopping and Exchange
51

CHAPTER THREE
The Betrayal of Tradition, the Tradition of Betrayal
91

CHAPTER FOUR
The Subversive Mind of the Maker
131

CHAPTER FIVE
The Politics of Religion, the Religion of Politics
171

CHAPTER SIX
A Brief Subversive Conclusion
211

Notes
215

Index
235

ACKNOWLEDGMENTS

Subversive was ignited not only by the shocking insights of Dorothy L. Sayers but also by people who encouraged me to apply those insights to pressing religious and political issues today. Acquainted with my first book, *Writing Performances: The Stages of Dorothy L. Sayers* (2004), Gina Dalfonzo asked me to write a short essay for *Christianity Today* about Sayers's contemporary relevance. Published in June 2018, the essay caught the attention of Emily King at Fortress Press, who suggested I consider composing a book on various ways Sayers might speak to people in our own era. By providing helpful feedback to my first draft, Emily has made this a much better book. Any remaining deficiencies are my own.

Subversive has also benefitted from invigorating conversations with colleagues at Wheaton College. I especially want to thank Tiffany Eberle Kriner for asking me to present an early chapter from *Subversive* at a college Humanities Colloquium, where I received encouraging and helpful responses. Several attending the colloquium went above and beyond the call of duty: Timothy Larsen met with me to discuss nuances about Christian history in my second chapter; Laura Yoder agreed to read and respond to my fifth chapter; and Christine Colón energized my thought, not only in multiple conversations, but also through her two books on Sayers. In addition to my colleagues, Sayers scholar Kathryn Wehr guided my understanding tremendously.

Equally important were the practical help and emotional support of the staff at the Marion E. Wade Center at Wheaton, which houses the world's most comprehensive collection of published and unpublished letters, papers, and books by and about Sayers. Wade Associate Director Marjorie Mead, herself a Sayers scholar, helped me get permissions to quote Sayers; Wade Office Coordinator Shawn Mrakovich, along with her husband, Pete, drew my attention to unpublished documents in which Sayers grapples with political issues, and Shawn also helped construct the index; Wade Archivist Laura Schmidt made available to me every published and unpublished Sayers item I needed; Aaron Hill, editor of the Wade journal, *VII*, constructed the chart for chapter 4 and encouraged conversations about Sayers for the Wade Center podcast, which he produces; Wade work-study student Leah McMichael helped with proofreading and citations. Finally, Operations Manager Mary Lynn Uitermarkt, Office Assistant Hope Grant, and Cataloguer Jill Walker provided listening ears and words of encouragement. I am fortunate to work with such an intelligent and conscientious team at the Wade Center, where I serve as codirector with my husband, C. S. Lewis scholar David C. Downing. He is my prime source of happiness, not only in the job, but for life itself.

INTRODUCTION
THE MURDER OF GOD

When Dorothy L. Sayers died in 1957, C. S. Lewis wept. Though she sometimes sharply criticized his opinions, Lewis delighted in Sayers's ability to communicate subversive perceptions in snappy, sometime hilarious ways, even if at his expense. In fact, when asked near the end of his life to name authors that influenced his spiritual life, Lewis identified four: two specialists on mysticism, G. K. Chesterton, and Dorothy L. Sayers.[1]

So why is C. S. Lewis a household name in the US, while Sayers remains largely unknown? Born five years apart, both achieved honors while students at Oxford University; both wrote best-selling novels while remaining serious about high-level scholarship; both influenced thousands of people to follow Jesus through 1940s radio broadcasts; both were awarded honorary doctorates; both have been praised by professional theologians for their provocative advocacy of Christian faith. Students at Oxford University and UC Berkeley were writing theses about Sayers long before Lewis became the focus of university study. It's no wonder that Lewis called Sayers "the first person of importance who ever wrote me a fan letter."[2] What happened to that importance?

By the end of this book, I hope to have answered these questions. But first I mean to intensify them by demonstrating that Sayers is even more relevant today than when Lewis wept over her death. *Subversive* explores and celebrates Sayers's theological brilliance, showing how her searing insight and cheeky wit can enlighten not only hesitant seekers but also long-time Christians in the twenty-first century. As the label *evangelical* alienates more and more people in our own era, Sayers can guide Christians through cultural minefields, providing direction to those wary of belief and weary of evangelical language.

The Mocking of Christ

Though she never renounced her childhood faith, Sayers felt the wariness and weariness many report today. She would perfectly understand twenty-first century *nones*: the name given to younger generations who mark "none" on official forms asking them to identify their religion.[3] Like many nones churched in their youth, Sayers often found liturgy "dreary beyond description," considering Psalm 23—"The Lord is my shepherd"—to be "rather smarmy."[4] During her adolescence she thought all too many Christians she encountered to be overbearing, judgmental, and narrow-minded. Glad that her college at Oxford University did not require chapel attendance, she wrote letters home asking her mother to send cigarettes, not spiritual advice. And when a relative urged her to join the Christian Social Union at Oxford, she was disgusted by the idea of joining a bunch of do-gooders. Married in her early thirties, she did not have a Christian wedding, tying the knot with an older divorced man in a civil ceremony to which her parents were not invited. When she thought that an "evangelical minister" might have influence over her young son, she told his caretaker, "if he shows any signs of being religious, I wash my hands of him."[5]

A poem Sayers wrote during her teenage years expresses how many adolescents feel today. Called "The Gargoyle," it describes a carved figure at the end of a church rain gutter that spouts water through its open mouth. Comparing the gargoyle with a preacher who "Spouts at his weary flock inside," she concludes, "I like the gargoyle best," since preachers can be "awful dampers when they're dry."[6]

Sayers's criticism of Christian practices was far less playful by her mid-twenties. In a dramatic poem called "The Mocking of Christ" (1918), she presents various ways so-called believers have treated Jesus throughout history. Inspired by the verse that states "where two or three are gathered in my name, I am there among them" (Matthew 18:20), the poem shows Jesus in the presence of people who do self-serving things in his name. For example, when a medieval pope fights a king over political power, both accidentally punch Jesus as they come to blows. After wresting control from the church, the king proclaims, "Who keeps quiet and serves the King / Can't go wrong in anything": another way of saying "I am the best leader for your country and will tolerate no criticism." Later in the poem, a similar antagonism arises between two patriots, both of whom claim that Jesus endorses their opposing political causes. As the nationalists argue about which party is more Christian, Jesus is splattered by their spit, thus mimicking mockers at the foot of the cross.[7]

In addition to politics, "The Mocking of Christ" satirizes religious commitments. Sayers has a Protestant preacher hand Jesus a Bible while telling him to only say "what we've always heard," thus turning Jesus into a supporter of the status quo. She continues in that vein with a clergyman who sets a cup of tea in Christ's hand, followed by someone who pats him on the back after giving him a cricket bat and pads. Jesus, Sayers makes clear, has been reduced to an excuse for polite socializing and feel-good camaraderie: either a comforting presence at church functions or one of the guys trotted out to help the home team win. Like someone who "parts Christ's hair in the middle," they have groomed a compliant savior who will challenge nothing.[8]

Because "The Mocking of Christ" mocked Christians in her own day, Sayers anticipated blowback, warning her parents about the volume of poetry, *Catholic Tales and Christian Songs,* in which the piece was to appear. Because some of her poems align Christian truth with pagan imagery, Sayers suspected that traditionalist "mugwumps" would consider her poetry blasphemous. Indeed, some readers were "shocked" by her "Black Magic style." However, rather than worry over the controversy, Sayers enjoyed shocking others, going so far as to ask a close friend to ignite a scandal by fabricating a letter to the *Church Times* denouncing the book. Her primary motivation was to have her collection of poems sell "like wildfire."[9] At this early stage of life, Sayers enjoyed being subversive more for the fame she might achieve than in order to help others intelligently grapple with their faith.

Subversive Christianity

When her faith was reenergized in middle age, Sayers did not change much in her desire to shock Christians, still disgusted by the way they had "certified" Jesus to be "meek and mild," thus turning the "Lion of Judah" into a "household pet for pale curates and pious old ladies": a well-trained pet trotted out to wag support for favored projects and policies, religious as well as political.[10] Her motivation, however, was now very different. Rather than bringing attention to herself, her chief goal was to subvert a warped understanding of the Gospel message. She recognized that all too many people consider Christianity to be a "prim tea-party, reserved for a very respectable and spiritually-minded upper class—quite regardless of the fact that Jesus Himself was notorious for the vulgar and shocking company He kept."[11]

Keeping vulgar and shocking company herself—actually delivering a lecture in 1936 called "The Importance of Being Vulgar"—Sayers can speak to those who have soured toward Christianity today; she understands where they are coming from. Disturbed by believers who regard protecting traditional cultural practices as the primary goal of the faith, Sayers chose to instead follow the example of Jesus, who, as she put it, "insulted respectable clergymen," defied "sacrosanct and hoary regulations," and asked "disagreeably searching questions that could not be answered by rule of thumb."[12] Not surprisingly, her subversive approach to Christianity outraged rule-of-thumb traditionalists all over England, much as Jesus outraged the scribes and Pharisees of his day.

Sayers knew that Christ came not to conserve the past but to convert the present. And she practiced what she preached. When invited by the Archbishop of York to speak to a national gathering of Christian leaders in 1941, she proceeded to deliver an address in which she described Christians as "tiresome, stupid, selfish, quarrelsome, pig-headed, and infuriating."[13] She knew, however, that she exemplified the list as much as anyone else. That is the very reason Sayers believed Christianity to be true, for it establishes that redemption "doesn't depend on us."[14] Despairing over Christians who imply otherwise, she challenged gargoyle-like believers who either dribble out reassuring platitudes or else drench society with rhetoric running off roofs of contemporary political platforms.

We have much to learn from Sayers about the relevance of Christianity to people suspicious of roof-stained waters. Having marginalized belief in her own life for decades, she can help us understand and address the cultural marginalization of Christianity in our own era. In fact, something she wrote in 1941 could have been written yesterday: "People of intelligence have drifted into the agnostic camp, and the world has become persuaded that it is impossible for any person with brains to be a Christian."[15] However, rather than denounce skeptics who seem to have murdered God, Sayers chose to build bridges between Christ and culture, having come to love them both. Passionately believing that faith in a Trinitarian God not only makes sense intellectually but also celebrates art and beauty, she despaired when her fellow Christians seemed more interested in maintaining the status quo than in changing lives—including their own.

An epigraph Sayers placed at the beginning of "The Mocking of Christ" summarizes her concern about Christianity, a concern she addressed for most of her life:

So man made God in his own image.
THE BOOK OF GENESIS (adapted)

Sayers's sly *adapted* tells it all: Christians have adapted their faith in order to maintain cultural practices and political agendas that make them feel most comfortable. Rather than adapting faith to legitimize the status quo, Sayers encourages adopting a faith so filled with trust in God that cultural change can be joyously engaged rather than fearfully denounced.

Male and Female God Created Them

Sayers saw the need to subvert cultural practices and political agendas due, in part, to her gender. Whereas Genesis 1:27 explicitly states that both males and females are created in the image of God, Christians in her day seemed more interested in making God in their image: as an endorser of male privilege. Though she did all the same work as her male peers at Oxford University, surpassing most by earning the highest honors in her discipline, Sayers was not granted a degree when she completed her studies in 1915. The university considered degrees unnecessary for women, if not inappropriate, since a woman's primary role in life was to train children, either as mothers or teachers.

Sayers dutifully followed the cultural script, getting a job as a teacher soon after leaving Oxford. But she hated it so much that she left after several terms. Returning to the city of Oxford—the place that fueled her intellect if not rewarded it—Sayers interned for a publisher while her father supported her. University policy changed only after the Great War decimated the male population, turning women into an attractive source of revenue.[16] In 1920, Sayers was part of the first group of women in history to be given degrees retroactively by Oxford, and she was awarded a BA and MA simultaneously in recognition of all she had achieved.

University policy reflects the assumptions of an entire society. As questions of female suffrage started roiling England in the late nineteenth century, Queen Victoria argued that "woman's rights" were "dangerous & unchristian & unnatural."[17] It is easy to smirk at the quaintness—and downright irony—of the Queen's position. What Sayers would later consider most disturbing, however, is the Queen's use of Christianity as an excuse for resisting change. Though Sayers had proven her intelligence at Oxford University and became key to the success of a London advertising firm that had hired her in 1922, she could not vote until she turned thirty years old: a law that applied to all women awarded Oxford degrees until the passage of Britain's Equal Franchise Act in 1928.

It is no wonder that Sayers jumped at the chance to pose as "the leader of a Suffragette demonstration" when recruited by a famous fashion historian for a 1950 show attended by British royalty.[18] Nevertheless, she refused to call herself a feminist, believing in practicing women's rights more than in preaching them. She knew that adamant preachers all too often lob alienating clichés that merely bounce off shields held high by protectors of convention. Sayers turned toward more subversive tactics, employing outrageous metaphors and biting wit to catch people off guard, as in her essays "Are Women Human?" (1938) and "The Human-Not-Quite-Human" (1941), both eventually published in her appropriately titled book *Unpopular Opinions* (1946). Rather than attacking people, however, Sayers attacks language, exposing how conventional terminology, spouted by gargoyle-like Christians on both the left and the right sides of the controversy, drowns out critical thinking.

In 1941, after a symposium called "The Emancipated Woman Comes of Age" appeared in *Christendom: A Journal of Christian Sociology*, Sayers wrote the editor to say that symposium contributors failed to fully capture the subtleties of the "woman question." After pulling threads that had been woven into "Are Women

Human?," she ends her long letter using a cheeky metaphor: "the Church must pull her socks up and introduce a spot of reality into this controversy."[19] Rather than leave it at that, Sayers proceeded to knit new socks for the church, writing an essay called "The Human-Not-Quite-Human" that the editor published in *Christendom* two months later. This time she went beyond "Are Women Human?" (written for a women's society) in order to explicitly address slouchy-socked Christians. And she held up their namesake as exemplar, delineating the shocking way Jesus treated women:

> A prophet and teacher who never nagged at them, never flattered or coaxed or patronised; who never made arch jokes about them, . . . who took their questions and arguments seriously; who never mapped out their sphere for them, never urged them to be feminine or jeered at them for being female. . . . There is no act, no sermon, no parable in the whole Gospel that borrows its pungency from female perversity; nobody could possibly guess from the words and deeds of Jesus that there was anything "funny" about women's nature.[20]

Constantly challenging the status quo, Jesus became Sayers's model for subversive Christianity. Unfortunately, as she explains on the same page in "The Human-Not-Quite-Human," Christians "to this day" fail to follow the example of their proclaimed Lord and Savior, preferring convention to change.

The Christian-Not-Quite-Christian

Sayers once compared someone who tries to protect Christianity from new ideas and practices to an old-fashioned grandmother trying to ward off an aggressive interviewer who is asking difficult questions of God: "I see her, deeply reverent in black bombazine, standing protectively between the pushing interviewer and the frail and aged figure of God in a bath-chair: 'Now, don't you speak rough to Him—He's very old and shaky, and I wouldn't answer for the consequences.'"[21] Sayers's point, of course, is the opposite: the Creator of the universe, who willingly suffered torture and crucifixion, can handle new ideas and practices as well as difficult questions about the relevance of Christianity to contemporary culture. As far as Sayers was concerned, a vibrant faith is a living and growing faith. It characterizes people that trust a strong and dynamic God rather than those that desperately seek to protect "old and shaky" traditions.

That doesn't mean she lets progressive Christians from her time off the hook, many of whom were not that much different from the deeply reverent grandmother. These Christians place Jesus in the bath-chair: though old and shaky after two thousand years, their Christ models godly human behavior better than any other human being. His divine spark must therefore be protected from pushing interviewers who buy into all that superstitious mumbo-jumbo about miracles. Sayers summarizes their position by saying, "Jesus was a good man—so good as to be called the Son of God. . . . He was meek and mild and preaches a simple religion of love and pacifism. He had no sense of humor." And she goes on to explain that such demythologizers, as they are known, assume anything in the Bible endorsing miracles must have been added later.[22] These so-called progressives therefore differ very little from fundamentalist Christians, picking and choosing what they want to believe in the Bible while discounting anything that makes them uncomfortable or fails to fit their worldview.

Sayers repeatedly challenged people from both the right and the left, protectors of traditional practices as well as promoters of change, disgusted by those who made no attempt to understand the doctrine they wanted to either conserve or undermine. And to those who dismissed Christianity altogether, she said, "If we are going to disbelieve a thing, it seems on the whole to be desirable that we should first find out what, exactly, we are disbelieving."[23] Nevertheless, she empathized with their disbelief, knowing that they had internalized a warped view of God. Whereas some regard God as old and shaky, others seem to endorse an arbitrary tyrant. The latter assume that God

> created the world and imposed on man conditions impossible of fulfillment; He is very angry if these are not carried out. He sometimes interferes by means of arbitrary judgment and miracles, distributed with a good deal of favoritism. He . . . is always ready to pounce on anybody who . . . is having a bit of fun. He is rather like a dictator, only larger and more arbitrary.[24]

Though Sayers is being sardonic, many Christians as well as skeptics seem to have inherited this view, the only difference being that Christians genuinely believe Jesus is the only one who can palliate God and therefore "if you want anything done, it is best to apply to Him."[25] Sayers would rather have both kinds of people apply themselves to learning the history of what they are accepting or rejecting.

Though dismayed by people "who heartily dislike and despise Christianity without having the faintest notion what it is,"[26] Sayers got downright irate when Christians turned the subversive truth of Christ's crucifixion into comfortable platitudes. Such believers seem to endorse Marx's famous description of religion: the opiate of the masses. Going to church to get their fix of feel-good religion, they numb their brains, turning Christianity into a numbskull religion. Educating people—from the right and the left, traditionalists as well as progressives—therefore became one of Sayers's most passionate goals.

Subverting Simplistic Thinking

Readers, beware. As Sayers warns one of her correspondents, "I have a way of upsetting people by what I do say."[27] She had a tendency to shock people not just by exposing their simplistic thinking, but by forcefully drawing attention to the subversive truth of the church's most ancient doctrines. Christians, she notes, are not called to denounce the murder of God; they are instead called to celebrate the "murder of God"[28] by witnessing to the fact that the crucified Jesus was God Incarnate:

> The story is a shocking one, even by human standards; but because its brutality is disguised for the common man by stereotyped expressions which have lost their power to shock, he accepts with mild complacency facts which ought to startle and horrify him like a blow in the face. If we cannot give him that blow in the face, what are we there for?[29]

Like a boxer wearing gloves stuffed with orthodox theology, Sayers repeatedly takes blows at Christian complacency—often sustaining black eyes from Christians who prefer stereotypical religious vocabularies to horrifying truths. Battling opponents from both the right and the left, Sayers called Christians to join her in the ring for a feistier faith:

Let us, in Heaven's name, drag out the Divine Drama from under the dreadful accumulation of slipshod thinking and trashy sentiment heaped upon it, and set it on an open stage to startle the world into some sort of vigorous reaction. If the pious are the first to be shocked, so much the worse for the pious.[30]

Indeed, so much the worse.

Subversive Then and Now

During the last decade of her life, Sayers had two primary passions: translating Dante's *Divine Comedy* for Penguin Books and participating in the Society of St. Anne, which hosted lectures about the relationship between Christ and culture as well as debates between believers and skeptics. Both projects brought out the best in Sayers, her incisive intellect delighting in the subversive truths of Christianity. In fact, what Sayers says about Dante, who has helped people see Christian truth through an imaginatively original lens, could adeptly describe her, once the pronouns are changed: "Beware of her. If you once come under the spell she will haunt your imagination, lay violent hands on your theology, intrude into your sermons and seep through your most casual conversation like a dye."[31] Readers are once again forewarned. Sayers, like Dante, "was anything but a docile member of the flock, and was quite prepared to teach orthodoxy to the Vatican."[32] As she explains to a skeptic not long before she fell in love with *The Divine Comedy*, "Christianity does and will challenge almost every conviction you have. That is its business. So don't blame me—You have been warned!"[33] Carrying a similar warning,

Subversive grapples with the shocking ways Sayers affirms ancient orthodoxy, illustrating how she raises Christian doctrine up out of a bath-chair in order to communicate its subversive truths.

Sayers can speak not only to those who believe doctrine about the murder of God, but also to those who despair that "Christians seem to be getting very savage" of late. In a statement that could have appeared on the opinion page of yesterday's newspaper, she writes,

> Today, the general feeling seems to be that we are everywhere over-run by Christians, who with brazen effrontery chatter on the roof, swarm in at the windows, snatch the meat from men's mouths and infants from the cradle, and are altogether grown so impudent and mischievous as to need destroying, like the rats of Hamelin, before they eat the place up.[34]

Rather than eat the place up, Sayers would have Christians offer the bread of heaven. Rather than snatch infants from the cradle, Sayers would have believers encourage new birth in Christ. *Bread of heaven* and *born again* are ancient phrases; but Sayers helps us to see their truth in subversive ways, as in her statement to theater producer Maurice Browne: "Christianity is as plain and common as bread."[35] By giving us new perspectives on the ways Christians themselves have warped the Gospel message, she confronts us with the continuing relevance of her epigraph to "The Mocking of Christ": "So humans made God in their own image."

It is hard to know whether Sayers would have been shocked by problems in twenty-first century American culture, like gun-toting adolescents killing schoolchildren or pornography available on multiple screens in any home. After all, she lived through one of the most degrading times in recent history, wherein Hitler inspired thousands of Christians to accept and support the brutal deportation and execution of innocent people. Whether shocked by our times or not, she would want us to focus our attention on the shock of the old: ancient doctrine about God's offer of forgiveness, even for the most despicable of sins, through the death and resurrection of Christ. As she once put it, "To make of His story something that could neither startle, nor shock, nor terrify, nor excite, nor inspire a living soul is to crucify the Son of God afresh and put Him to an open shame."[36] It is a subversive story about the murder of God—and what we decide to do about it.

CHAPTER ONE
THE SHOCK OF THE NEW

When someone alludes to shocking language in the twenty-first century, most people assume it is a reference to f-bombs bundled together with other colorful four-letter words into a bouquet of vulgarity. A disturbing style implies excessively explicit images, from graphic sex to gruesome violence. Dorothy L. Sayers was shocking and disturbing in a different way. Rather than taking the name of Christ in vain, Sayers's shocking language compelled thousands to take seriously the name of Jesus—but not before scandalizing pious Christians, whose protests over Sayers's disturbing style generated a nationwide "uproar."[1]

The controversy was ignited by twelve radio plays Sayers wrote for the British Broadcasting Corporation (BBC radio)—almost forty years before BBC television broadcast a series called *The Shock of the New*. While the latter series, written by art critic Robert Hughes, explored modern art and people's outrage over its defiance of centuries-old conventions, Sayers's BBC series dramatized the life, death, and resurrection of Jesus, itself outraging people by its defiance of centuries-old conventions. Because her ability to appall numerous Christians happened at a time very similar to our own, Sayers can provide us with blueprints for culture-changing Christianity.

In order to build from those blueprints, we first need to understand how Sayers developed into someone who could shock an entire generation—like modernist painters. At the same time, we need to respect Sayers's sentiments, which she repeated often: "I don't approve much of biographical details."[2] Disturbed by the way listeners, readers, and viewers seem more interested in artists' lives than in the creative work to which those artists dedicated themselves, Sayers wants us to concentrate on what she communicates in and through her writings, not on incidentals about her personal life.

Sayers as Mystery Author

Sayers gained celebrity due to her best-selling detective fiction, with her first novel published in 1923. One of the founding members of London's prestigious Detection Club, established by and for successful detective fiction authors, Sayers delighted in the organization's formal dinners and initiation rites, which included a human skull—named Eric—that was ceremoniously carried into the assembly room on a cushion. In 1949, she became the Detection Club's third president (the first was G. K. Chesterton), relishing her responsibilities until she died in 1957, at which time Agatha Christie took over. Sayers's famous fictional creation, amateur sleuth Lord Peter Wimsey, parallels Christie's fastidiously dressed, music-loving detective Hercule Poirot more than Chesterton's self-effacing, Jesus-loving Father Brown, however. Indeed, Sayers's Lord Peter respects Christianity but is decidedly non-religious, valuing the beautiful form of church architecture and liturgy more than its spiritual content.

Sayers, however, is much more subversive than Agatha Christie, perhaps explaining why the latter is better known. One specialist in detective fiction notes that Sayers's very first novel, *Whose Body?*, "shocks because it takes the detective story as it had been written and stands it on its head; the book manages to mock the conventions of the form and to become a new kind of detective story."[3] Sayers moved from mocking the conventions of Christianity, as described in the preceding chapter, to mocking the conventions of detective fiction. And it brought her the celebrity she sought.

Nevertheless, like Agatha Christie, Sayers became increasingly impatient with the fictional detective who made her famous. Christie, though reaching the point where she considered Poirot "insufferable" and "tiresome," kept him going for readers' sakes— and perhaps for her own financial sake.[4] In contrast, Sayers decided to "get rid of" Lord Peter by "marrying him off" to a woman detective novelist accused of murdering her live-in lover.[5] Ironically, in the process of developing the character of that fictional novelist, Harriet Vane, Sayers discovered that she needed to change Peter in order to make him worthy of a creative, independent woman whose intelligence was considerably more impressive than her beauty. Sayers, in other words, was willing to subvert her own efforts at subversion.

In the process of changing Lord Peter for Harriet's sake, Sayers continued to challenge the conventions of detective fiction. As Harriet slowly becomes Sayers's protagonist over the course of several novels, she takes center stage of a detective novel that has no murder. This move in *Gaudy Night* (1935) was unusual, especially since the ultimate mystery Harriet must solve is whether a woman can balance a career with marriage in 1930s England. Sally Munt, a professor of media and cultural studies, argues that Sayers almost single-handedly changed the genre of detective fiction with *Gaudy Night*.[6] Challenging contemporary cultural constructions of gender as well as genre, Sayers ultimately subverted the status quo of detective fiction itself. This helps explain why she is not well-known today: readers, whether of the Bible or of detective fiction, prefer the status quo.

Facing the Architecture of Christianity

Sayers's defiance of the status quo in her fiction reflects a basic truth of Christian orthodoxy: God desires change. After all, the word *conversion* means "with turning"—turning to face a new direction—and *sanctification* indicates ongoing change to greater Christlikeness. But Sayers had a long way to go before applying those words to her own spiritual life. Fortunately, she was open to change.

While still in the midst of converting her detective novels to more culturally relevant content, Sayers received a request to change the direction of her writing altogether. In 1936, she was asked to follow in the footsteps of poet T. S. Eliot by writing a play to be performed in Canterbury Cathedral. It was a startling invitation. After all, T. S. Eliot was considered a genius by the intellectual elite who celebrated avant-garde poetic styles while looking down on best-selling fiction. Fans of Eliot disdained popular writers like Sayers, who, as far as they were concerned, had sold out to the marketplace by writing bestsellers. Though Sayers had published two books of poetry early in her career, T. S. Eliot wrote intellectual verse that defied the Victorian poetic style to which Sayers was accustomed. How could she possibly compete? Nevertheless, like Harriet Vane facing her fears about marrying an elite aristocrat, Sayers faced her fears about marrying her writing skills to a more elite project. Less than a year after the publication of Harriet's "yes" to Lord Peter's marriage proposal, Sayers said "yes" to the daunting Canterbury proposal. And, like a healthy marriage, the decision changed her life for the better.

Because the Canterbury play was supposed to relate to the cathedral's history, Sayers chose as her protagonist William of Sens, the architect hired to rebuild the cathedral choir after it was destroyed by fire in 1174 CE. Significantly, she made the historical William similar in personality to her fictional Lord Peter: passionate about solving problems, confident in his talents, discrete about his sexual liaisons, and respectful of but not committed to Christianity. Most importantly, Lord Peter and William of Sens both value what Sayers had come to call the "integrity" of work: a commitment to doing the best possible job in the vocation to which one feels called.

The integrity of work, in fact, helps solve several mysteries in *Gaudy Night*—including the mystery of marriage. Early in the novel Harriet explains why marriage is problematic for her as a university alumna: "I'm sure one should do one's *own job*, however trivial, and not persuade one's self into doing somebody else's, however noble." It is a problem solved when Harriet discovers that Peter, though part of the nobility, values the integrity of *her* job as well as his own. Significantly, Sayers gives similar words to William of Sens, who wants the cathedral treasurer to "allow me to know my *own job*."[7] Another character in the play, the cathedral historian, later confirms that William "has never cheated the

Church of a single penny, and never would. He thinks of nothing, lives for nothing, but the integrity of his work."[8]

Despite the similarities between Lord Peter and William of Sens, the Canterbury play forced Sayers to consider how the integrity of work applies to a wholly different kind of mystery: the mystery that inspired the construction of Canterbury Cathedral in the first place. Having been a member of the Anglican Church her whole life, Sayers believed Christianity to be true. But applying that truth to her detective novels, let alone to her daily life, had interested her little. Now, twenty-five years after going off to university, Sayers felt compelled to think more deeply about what it meant to dedicate one's work to the church. Unlike Lord Peter, then, who changes by humbling himself before a talented woman committed to the integrity of work, Sayers has William of Sens change by humbling himself before almighty God. Doing so, she moved from secular to sacred motivation in her characters' behavior.

By fleshing out William's commitment to work, Sayers was forced to reassess her own commitment to work, especially as her marriage to a veteran with post-traumatic stress disorder was becoming increasingly difficult. She came to realize that living for the integrity of work can lead to pride in one's abilities, cutting one off from the needs of others and supplanting the reign of God in one's life. Indeed, she has William make the outrageous claim that, when it comes to architecture, he surpasses not only everyone else in Canterbury, but also God. As he is lifted by ropes to the top of a soaring arch to place the keystone in his new construction, Sayers symbolizes his desire to have all eyes below lifted to see his craftsmanship more than to praise the God to whom the arch points. The rope breaks, however, and the devastating fall permanently cripples William. Pride quite literally goes before a fall in Sayers's play (see Proverbs 16:18).

Knowing her Bible well, like most Oxford-educated people of her era, Sayers understood that the attempt to "be like God," as in the Garden of Eden (Genesis 3:5), causes the Fall: a plummet into the crippling power of self-serving sin. Her play, though set in the twelfth century, thus speaks to all times and places, exposing the sin of arrogant self-aggrandizing leaders who think they can rise above common ethics by constructing architecture according to their own blueprints, whether literal walls or symbolic systems. Indeed, letters show that Sayers was appalled by Hitler's rise to power as she was writing the play. But, at the same time, she couldn't help thinking about how her own life had been crippled by elevating her desires above common sense, if not God's will, as in her sudden marriage to a divorcé she barely knew. The words she gave to the crippled William started to become her own: "God hath changed my mind."[9]

Changing Her Mind: A Zeal for Christianity

Called *The Zeal of Thy House*, Sayers's Canterbury play was an amazing success. Its theological profundity, enhanced by humor and provocative references to William's sexual life, drew audiences to over one hundred performances after it went on tour. Sayers's focus on the architect's fall lifted her up to a soaring arch of Christian fame. However, having been instructed by William's example, she directed the limelight to the integrity of her work rather than to herself as a brilliant evangelist. As she told someone years later, "I never, so help me God, wanted to get entangled in religious apologetics, or to bear witness for Christ, or to proclaim my faith to the world."[10]

Nevertheless, in order to promote *The Zeal of the House* as it opened in London, Sayers wrote an article, published in London's *Sunday Times* (April 3, 1938), titled "The Greatest Drama Ever Staged is the Official Creed of Christendom." In the piece she argues not only that Christ's death and resurrection are historical fact, but that Jesus shocked people during his life, especially people with political power. And she criticizes Christians for succeeding "to muffle up" the "shattering personality" of Jesus by surrounding him with religious "tedium."[11]

The church's muffling of Christ's subversive personality helps explain why, for decades, Sayers did not overtly identify herself with Christianity. She had no patience for tedium. It also helps explain why, today, Christians have turned their backs on a Jesus who has become the household pet of politicians: trotted out to support their agendas, though always kept on a leash. Having escaped the leash of conformist Christianity in her youth, Sayers was now arguing, as a secular detective novelist in a secular newspaper, that when Jesus died on the cross, it was God Almighty that was murdered. Though many people regard such an idea "rubbish," as she puts it, informed Christians consider it "revelation": Gospel truth, as it were. Neither group, however, has a right to call it tedious or "dull."[12]

Notice Sayers's tactics here: rather than perpetuate the polarization between believers and skeptics, she offered something both groups could agree on. *Whether one believed it or not*, the concept that the Creator of the universe could be murdered by pious people was shocking. Subverting polarized rhetoric by offering something that demanded mutual consent, Sayers forced *both* kinds of people to rethink the way they discuss "the terrifying assertion that the same God who made the world lived in the world and passed through the grave and gate of death." She followed up this assertion, published in another popular periodical that same month (April 1938), with defiance: "Show that to the heathen, and they may not believe it; but at least they may realize that here is something that a man might be glad to believe."[13]

People were stunned by Sayers's emphatic endorsement of Christian faith. Years later, Sayers summarized the effect of her articles: "That did it. Apparently the spectacle of a middle-aged female detective-novelist admitting publicly that the judicial murder of God might compete in interest with the Corpse in the Coal-Hole was the sensation for which the Christian world was waiting."[14] No one anticipated that Sayers would soon create a totally different kind of sensation: one that would outrage Christians. Whereas William of Sens ignited "a Scandal in the Cathedral" due to his arrogance,[15] Sayers ignited a scandal throughout Great Britain—not because she had fallen into pride, but because she had begun to deeply ponder what it means to follow the subversive example of Jesus Christ.

Born to Be Scandalous

Due to the success of *Zeal* and the sensation of her essays in popular periodicals, Sayers was invited to write another Canterbury play and a radio script about the birth of Jesus, even as numerous newspapers, journals, church groups, and social clubs started asking her to write and speak on Christian topics. In 1940 came her biggest commission yet: the BBC asked her to write the series of twelve radio plays about the life, death, and resurrection of Jesus.

Taking the commission very seriously, Sayers spent over a year rereading the Gospels—in the original Greek, no less—while studying Bible commentaries and histories of the era in order to give her scripts both historical accuracy and dramatic flair. Believing in the relevance of the message for all time, Sayers wanted to avoid what she called a "stained-glass-window" understanding of the Gospels, wherein biblical characters are merely "'sacred personages', standing about in symbolic attitudes," rather than flesh-and-blood humans like the rest of us. As she continues to explain in her introduction to the printed version of the scripts, "It is curious that people who are filled with horrified indignation whenever a cat kills a sparrow can hear that story of the killing of God told Sunday after Sunday and not experience any shock at all." Finding comfort in hearing the same old stories over and over, Christians have lost the ability to see Jesus and His disciples as *really* real people."[16] Protective of the Bible's stained-glass beauty, they tend to look *at* Scripture rather than *through* it.

In contrast, Sayers wanted her radio plays to reveal, like a clear window, the subversive truth of Christianity, especially the fact that "God was executed by people painfully like us."[17] Knowing that most of Christ's followers were working class, she enhanced authenticity by making some of the disciples sound like blue-collar laborers in her own day. When Roman soldiers spoke, she had them use military language familiar to a country in the midst of World War II. Without changing the fundamental Gospel message, she made up scenes to contextualize Christ's parables and to dramatize the lives of those who listened to his sermons and witnessed his miracles, justifying the inclusion of fictional incidents by noting that not everything

Jesus said and did was recorded in the Gospels. After all, John ends his Gospel saying, "there are also many other things that Jesus did; if every one of them were written down, I suppose that the world itself could not contain the books that would be written" (John 21:25).

By December of 1941 Sayers's radio plays were ready for serial broadcast. The BBC hosted a press conference to advertise the new series, during which Sayers read snippets from her scripts, collectively titled *The Man Born to Be King*. That did it. Apparently the spectacle of a middle-aged female detective-novelist giving a new spin to the Gospel message was the sensation for which the world of journalism was waiting. Reporters turned the BBC radio plays into the scandal de jour. When news broke about Sayers's unconventional approach to biblical material, outraged Christians mounted a censorship campaign, writing the Archbishop of Canterbury and Prime Minister Winston Churchill to demand the plays be taken off the air. Though reviled in the press and receiving abusive phone calls, Sayers stood by the integrity of her work, refusing to back down. The BBC supported her, holding its ground as well. Nevertheless, even after the plays began to air, Sayers got anonymous letters of insult, with one postcard addressing her as "You nasty old sour-puss."[18]

Christian Resistance to Change

So why did Christians all over England, including the Protestant Truth Society, which maintains offices in London to this day, try to censor the plays? The answer is complicated but ultimately applicable to the communication of subversive Christianity in our own time.

Problem 1: Portraying Jesus

By producing a dramatic rendition of Christ's life, Sayers and the BBC were challenging a three-hundred-year-old British law prohibiting theatrical impersonations of Jesus. As Sayers's friend Barbara Reynolds notes, "At this period it was not permitted to represent any Person of the Trinity directly on stage or in films"— a prohibition not repealed in England until 1965.[19]

The law reflects Puritan efforts to purify Christianity by removing all taints of Roman Catholic and secular decadence from their Protestant country. Not only did seventeenth-century Puritans shut down secular theaters, including those performing Shakespeare, they suppressed Miracle and Mystery Plays, based on Bible stories and saints' lives, that were acted out on village streets in various parts of England. Written by pre-Reformation priests, the subversive plays celebrated the Feast of Corpus Christi, a holiday honoring the doctrine of transubstantiation, which established that the blessed Eucharist bread and wine transform into the blood and body of Christ: the Corpus Christi. Like their Protestant forebears a century earlier, the Puritans denounced transubstantiation, and they outlawed actors from transforming into the body of Christ—the corpus of Christi—in dramas based on the Gospels.

Sayers and the BBC director of religious broadcasting, James Welch, discussed the centuries-old prohibition before proceeding with plans for the project, deciding that the disembodied voices of radio got around transubstantiated actors performing on stage. Nevertheless, the broadcasts were still considered subversive, with journalists of the day describing the BBC series as "the first time a radio impersonation of Christ has been attempted anywhere in the world."[20] One listener wrote in to say "Having had a Puritan upbringing, my feelings were entirely against a play on such a subject."[21] But Sayers and Welch hoped that radio performances of Gospel material might pave the way to change: that someday depictions of Jesus on British stage and screen could testify to the truth of God's gift of forgiveness. A tactic as applicable today as in the 1940s, Sayers and Welch challenged the religious status quo in order to advance the Gospel message.

Problem 2: Language

Sayers wanted her plays to reflect that Jesus was born not into the Bible but into history, that he lived and moved and had his being among people very similar to those in her own era. Believing that Jesus was "a man born to be king" over all human hearts—no matter the place, no matter the time—Sayers refused to use King James English for her characters, only occasionally allowing Jesus to quote familiar verses from what was at the time called "the Authorized Version." Furthermore, she had many characters, including Christ's disciples, speak common slang terms of her day. Worse, some of it was *American* slang! For example, when the disciple Matthew learns that another disciple has been cheated at the marketplace, he says, "Fact is, Philip my boy, you've been had for a sucker."[22] Read by Sayers at the press conference, it was this line that provided journalists with tinder to ignite a blazing controversy.

Overheated by Sayers's use of slang in broadcasts about Jesus, Christians wanted to torch the entire project. The Lord's Day Observance Society (LDOS) published a statement soon after the press conference, denouncing Sayers's "spoliation of the beautiful language of the Holy Scriptures which have been given by inspiration of the Holy Spirit."[23] Though not going so far as to proclaim, "If King James English was good enough for Jesus, it's good enough for us," one protester objected when Sayers's King Herod told his court "keep your mouths shut," arguing that anyone "so closely connected with our Lord" should not be using "such coarse expressions."[24]

Such protests seem laughable to us today, but their historical context should make us more sympathetic and hence more open to learning from the scandal.

Problem 3: Historical Context

The BBC had scheduled the press conference, when Sayers read from her colloquial scripts, for December 11, 1941—which ended up being three days after the Japanese bombed Pearl Harbor. Though Britain had been at war with Germany for over two years by then, the increasing strength of Axis powers naturally put citizens on edge. Sayers's unconventional language for plays about Jesus therefore seemed to attack the Christian harbor guarding the pearl of great price. And when people feel their way of life is being threatened, they cling to convention for spiritual comfort food, constructing walls to keep foreign people and foreign ideas from invading their mental dining rooms, often mounting counterattacks to protect life as they know it.

Indeed, Sayers likened the attacks on *The Man Born to Be King* to a war zone, writing to the BBC producer that if both their names were "mud when the fighting is over" then they would just have to "stick in the mud together and suffer for our convictions."[25] Two weeks later she wrote to James Welch, arguing that if those who originally approved the radio scripts "don't stand to their guns," they will look weak and ignorant. She then proceeded to quote Winston Churchill who, though brilliantly evacuating British troops from the Dunkirk beaches, nevertheless stated, "Wars are not won by evacuation." In other words, Sayers believed that to give up on the whole project by evacuating production crew from *The Man Born to Be King* would be conceding too much to the enemy. Assuring Welch that she trusted him to lead, if necessary, a withdrawal of broadcast personnel—"we can rely on you to make a Dunkirk of it"—she nevertheless told him that, by giving in to outraged Christians, "there will be a loss in armaments, baggage, and fighting-power" necessary to fulfill their goal of communicating the Gospel.[26] Wars are not won by evacuation.

BBC executives agreed with Sayers, and the plays continued to be broadcast after the first was aired on December 21, 1941. The third play, about the miracle at Cana and Christ's cleansing of the Temple, aired on February 8, 1942: the day Japanese troops invaded Singapore, Britain's largest military base in Southeast Asia. After Japan conquered the British stronghold a week later, once again traumatizing British citizens, incensed Christians proclaimed that the fall of Singapore was God's revenge for Sayers's sacrilegious radio plays.[27]

Learning in Wartime

How, then, might battles over *The Man Born to Be King* speak to our own era when secular culture seems to be at war with faith? It's easy to feel smug about the naïveté of 1940s Christians who sanctified King James English. Indeed, many passages from the 1611 King James Version that they wanted to protect were lifted straight from William Tyndale's 1526 translation of the Bible, an English translation that led Christians to burn Tyndale at the stake. After all, as everyone knew at the time, the sacred language of Scripture was Latin! They believed Tyndale was making war on the Bible, forcing it to conform to vulgar signs of English culture. In other words—other words quite literally—change that is reviled at one moment in history becomes sacred text centuries later.

In Sayers's case, it didn't take centuries. Due to the press-fed nationwide scandal, scores of people who rarely listened to religious programming, having little interest in Jesus and the Bible, tuned in just to get a taste of the controversy. What they ingested was a message of salvation that made sense to their slang-slinging lives. Sayers told C. S. Lewis that she got thousands of letters from wary listeners who told her that the BBC broadcasts inspired them to read the Bible with interest for the first time in their lives, that they finally understood the significance of the Gospel message, or that they had rededicated their lives to Christ. Only seven years after the initial scandal, Sayers's scripts were already being translated into Czech and Welsh. By 1954, *The Man Born to Be King* was required reading in Christian schools, and when the play cycle was rebroadcast in 1975, listeners had trouble believing that Christians in the early 1940s considered the plays offensive.[28] Lewis himself was so moved by the published version of *The Man Born to Be King* (1943) that he read it for his Lenten devotions every year until he died. Sayers was able to minister to thousands of people not in spite of but due to her shocking subversion of convention.

One listener adeptly articulated the value of what Sayers had done, writing to confirm the importance of making the scripts available in print form:

The very language you use "shocks" us out of worn conventional terms, and I know that the thousands of people who never dream of reading their Bible, let alone try to understand it, will be led to see the way of Christ as most necessary for our times. I can see our adolescents who drift away from tame Sunday School stories go for your book-to-be and read it and gain inspiration from it.[29]

Inspired by these and many other words of support, Sayers wrote an introduction to the print version of the plays in which she calls the demand for King James English a "singular piece of idolatry": "bibliolatry" as she puts it.[30] Then as now, many Christians idolized traditional language in and interpretations of the Bible that made them feel comfortable—protecting stained-glass depictions—more than they attempted to follow Christ's glass-shattering teaching.

Escalators of Change: Finding Footing in the Creeds

Sayers fully understood that new ideas and practices can be terrifying, as when she took her first escalator ride in 1915. When department stores first introduced escalators, store personnel stood by with brandy in hand, offering it to anyone who felt faint after riding the new-fangled contraptions. During her own first experience of a "moving staircase," as Sayers calls it, a friend held her arm, worried she might "get giddy." Sayers describes what next happened in amusing detail: "Suddenly an old lady pushed violently past me" while "muttering 'I must get down this thing quickly, I'm always sick if I don't,'" and she "hurled herself to the bottom in a series of goat-like leaps."[31] Today, of course, many of us make "goat-like leaps" on an escalator for the opposite reason: the device feels so annoyingly slow. Cultural innovations at their start often generate distress, making us feel as though safe ground is moving away too quickly. But over time we adjust, just as Christians adjusted to colloquial language in *The Man Born to Be King*.

After resisting Christian outrage for putting the voice of Jesus on the radio, Sayers kept moving up and beyond convention on the escalator of change. Four years after *The Man Born to Be King* controversy, she more explicitly defied Britain's three-hundred-year-old prohibition against actors playing Jesus. In *The Just Vengeance*, a 1946 play she once called "the best thing I've done,"[32] Sayers had an actor perform the character of Jesus on a live stage. Even though the stage was constructed inside Lichfield Cathedral, a place where the words of Jesus had been pronounced for centuries, Sayers once again had to battle protectors of the status quo. At one point she threatened to withdraw from the project, and, even after winning that battle, she found herself repeatedly sparring with the dean of the cathedral over elements in her script.[33] Based on an airman who was shot down during World War II, and who converses with the actor playing Jesus, the script admittedly subverted convention. But it worked. As Barbara Reynolds notes, "The play was scheduled to run for eleven days but the demand for seats was so great that the period was extended for another three."[34] Ten thousand people attended the performances, including the Archbishop of York and the mother of Queen Elizabeth, all of whom were shocked by the ancient Gospel message presented in a radical new way. Escalators of change can carry people to higher places. However, as Sayers would readily assert, to uncritically idealize change as a good in and of itself is just as naïve as uncritically resisting it. While discussing the stairway that leads Dante to the top of Purgatory, she admits that some people "make a fetish of progress."[35]

When it comes to a moving staircase, no matter how superbly crafted, an escalator will only be completely safe in stores having firm foundations. This lends significance to the opening line of a well-known hymn: "the church's one foundation is Jesus Christ her Lord." Those who sing that line with belief, however, must acknowledge that the "footings" of the foundation, as they are known, were poured by earnest followers of Christ in early centuries of the faith before the biblical canon was even finalized. Sayers repeatedly reminds people of this fact, sending them back to the original Creeds that grounded the nature of Christ: Jesus was both fully human and fully God. This is what Sayers considers "the distinguishing belief" of all Christian Churches; it is the foundation that cements together Roman Catholic, Eastern Orthodox, and Protestant believers.[36]

Rather than practicing "bibliolatry," then, Sayers insists that Christians ground escalators of change in the distinguishing beliefs formulated at the first four international meetings of church leaders, known as Ecumenical Councils. Though other councils were to follow, she, like C. S. Lewis, privileged the first four because they represented "the whole and undivided Church."[37] She felt so strongly about the importance of this undivided foundation that she wrote an entire play about the first Ecumenical Council at Nicaea, which launched the Nicene Creed. Even though it wasn't until the fourth council, held at Chalcedon in 451 CE, that Christians finalized what it meant for Jesus to be *fully human*, Sayers wanted to focus her attention on the initial ecumenical meeting, over a century earlier, which established that Jesus was *fully God*.

Called *The Emperor Constantine,* Sayers's play dramatizes what Christian histories tell us: convened by the Emperor Constantine in 325 CE, the First Council of Nicaea established that the murder of God was a foundational doctrine of Christianity. Proclaiming Jesus to be "God of God, Light of Light, true God of true God, begotten not made, being of one substance with the Father," the Council formulated their statement, the Nicene Creed, in response to the bibliolatry of Arius, an earnest follower of Jesus. As Sayers shows in her play, Arius used Scripture to make his argument that Christ was not one with God. After all, Jesus talks about his Heavenly *Father* in the Gospels, repeatedly calling himself the *Son* of God. Hence, as in any Father/Son relationship, Jesus must be subsequent to rather than one with God. Not only do the Gospels prove it, but the apostle Paul confirms it, telling the Colossians that Jesus is "the first*born* of all creation" (1:15). Though based on the Bible, this interpretation was declared heresy by the Council of Nicaea.

The Church's One Foundation

Clearly, understanding the essence of Christianity takes more than reading one's Bible, whether in Hebrew, Greek, Latin, or King James English. As Sayers well knew, the cement of the Bible didn't solidify until 397 CE: the year that the biblical canon was finalized at the Council of Carthage, which was more than seventy years after the Council at Nicaea declared Jesus and God to be one substance. Ancient Christian doctrine, in other words, provides the foundation upon which we build biblical interpretation. Indeed, when someone wrote Sayers asking for a "Scriptural sanction for the doctrine of the Trinity," Sayers challenged the very idea. Knowing that the word *Trinity* appears nowhere in the Bible, Sayers replied:

> Where is your Scriptural authority for the Scriptures them-
> selves? On what texts do you rely for the make-up of the
> Canon as we have it? Where, for example, does the Lord say
> that there are to be those four Gospels and no more? or that
> the *Revelation of Peter* and *The Shepherd of Hermas* are not
> authoritative—though the first was read in churches as early
> as the second century, and the second was included in the
> *Codex Sinaiticus* as late as the fourth century? The doctrine of
> the Trinity was worked out and formulated in the Church—
> the same Church that is the authority for the Canon itself.[38]

In other words, we must read Scripture in light of the doctrine of the Trinity, seeking illumination by the same Holy Spirit who inspired ancient church bishops in formulating that doctrine.

This does not mean Sayers disregarded the Bible. When one correspondent argued that "it is better for the Jews to remain unconverted," she called his position "unorthodox and difficult to reconcile with Scripture."[39] After all, she knew that followers of Christ attending the Ecumenical Councils relied on gospel accounts and letters from apostles as they established the funda-mental Creeds of Christianity. But she also knew that they had heated debates. Arguments arose at Ecumenical Councils because the Bible, then as now, is not self-interpreting. Anyone who claims to know the correct interpretation of Scripture—as did Arius—ultimately proclaims to know the mind of God, which is both arrogant and blasphemous.

Not coincidentally, Sayers gives Arius an obnoxiously arrogant personality in *The Emperor Constantine*. Arius condescendingly tells church leaders attending the council that he will defend his position "against those who are too illiterate to understand Greek, and too indolent to study the Scriptures." Like a politician who specializes in negative campaigning, he contemptuously disparages Christians from Rome in order to imply that anyone who disagrees with him must be stupid: "Our Latin friends who have no definite article in their woolly language may be excused for woolly thinking; but for those who speak Greek there is no excuse." As Janice Brown astutely summarizes, Sayers's Arius is "arrogant to the point of insolence."[40] Sayers would certainly be dismayed, though perhaps not surprised, by Christians today who wholeheartedly endorse arrogant politicians who act as though anyone who disagrees with them is a fool.

What especially disturbed Sayers, however, was the practice of picking and choosing Bible verses out of context in order to avoid the shock of the new, much as Arius and his followers resisted the shock of God's murder by highlighting passages that established Jesus as the *Son* of God. For such bibliolaters, the famous hymn might as well say "the church's one foundation is my denomination's interpretation of truth." Sayers, in contrast, would have us maintain that the church's one foundation is Jesus Christ, whose nature was worked out in the Ecumenical Councils and formulated in the ancient Creeds: statements of doctrine upon which we build the house of faith. If changes in culture do not undermine this solid foundation of Christianity, they must be prayerfully considered.

For an apt analogy, think of an historic house. In order to maintain the house for future generations, parts must be replaced as they rot and rust over time. Changing out the original roof, rafters, or beams of an old edifice is often necessary to keep it standing firm on its foundation. We might call it a "zeal for thy house." Indeed, it was zeal for the house of Christianity that inspired Martin Luther and led to the Protestant Reformation. Committed to the most ancient Creeds, Luther didn't want to destroy the house of Christianity; he instead wanted to replace doctrines and practices that had become rotten. Nevertheless, as with twentieth-century Christians who tried to censor Sayers for *The Man Born to Be King*, sixteenth-century Christians tried to censor Luther for his protests nailed to the door of a house of God. The Protestant Reformation illustrates the verse from Psalms that inspired Sayers: "It is zeal for your house that has consumed me; the insults of those who insult you have fallen on me" (Psalms 69:9).

Which Burning Heresy?

Insults were showered upon Sayers, Luther, and Tyndale by people so shocked by the new that they failed to see how all three wanted to preserve the foundation of Christianity. Though earnest followers of Christ, all three were reviled as heresy-spouting witches, with Tyndale treated like a witch quite literally when he was burned at the stake for ideas that most Protestants accept today as true. It is no wonder that skeptics often think of Christians as irrational heresy-hunters who consume with rhetorical fire anyone who disagrees with their religious or political positions.

So which heresies are the witch heresies? Sayers would answer by once again drawing our attention to the foundational footings poured by the first four Ecumenical Councils, made up of respected church leaders from Africa, Asia, and Europe who felt the need to distinguish heresy from orthodoxy. They knew that a foundation needs to be solid to allow for changes to the architecture built upon it. Their concern reminds me of my father's job as a mechanical engineer, for which he would often make surprise inspections at project sites. Having designed the heating, plumbing, and air conditioning for a school or hospital, he would show up unexpectedly, usually as builders were pouring the foundation. He did so to inspect pipes and ducts important for efficient plumbing and HVAC systems before conduits were covered up by concrete. Sometimes discovering that the builders, in order to save money, had failed to follow his specifications, he would ask them to pull up and replace the incorrect system. Builders often expressed anger over their wasted time and money, sometimes accusing my father of being an uptight legalist—much as people today accuse Christians committed to ancient Creeds as being inflexible. But my father's primary goal was to support the education of children and the healing of patients as effectively and as long as possible in schools and hospitals so well built that they could sustain change, such as the incorporation of a new wing or updated technology. My father didn't act entirely by himself; he was part of a community of architects, engineers, and contractors who gave well-educated *opinions* about "the integrity of [their] work," to borrow Sayers's phrase from *The Zeal of Thy House*. In contrast, builders who cut corners were making what might be called *heretical* choices that served their own best interests.

Significantly, the word *heresy* comes from a Greek root that means "choice": a heretic, in other words, is someone who *chooses* to believe something that does not fit the blueprints—what we might call the *dogma*—established by a community of well-informed designers. Even the word *dogma* is less dogmatic than people assume. As Sayers notes, the word for *dogma,* in both Greek and

Latin, means *opinion*: Christian dogma is "an opinion endorsed by the whole body" of believers.[41] She repeatedly alludes to heresies throughout her writings, knowing that a good foundation, whether containing the right-sized pipes or the best-shaped dogma, can allow for positive changes to the architecture of a hospital or of Christianity as the culture around it changes. It's all about zeal for God's house, not about personal *choices* over feel-good Christianity.

Repudiating feel-good spirituality, Sayers changed thousands of lives because she did not care at all whether people felt good about *her*; she cared, instead, about shocking people with the subversive truth of Christian dogma. As she told a publisher who asked her to write up her personal beliefs—to "set" them "down" in print for publication—"Nothing would induce me to 'set down my religious beliefs and convictions.' Setting down what I understand to be the church's beliefs and convictions is a different matter."[42] In other words, Sayers believed people should embrace Christianity not because a celebrity novelist and playwright like herself had done so, but because ancient followers of Jesus "set down" a foundation so true that it has supported changes to the house of Christianity for thousands of years.

Repeatedly denouncing what she calls "the personal angle," Sayers appeals to the integrity of church doctrine rather than her own personal integrity when it comes to issues of faith.[43] As she later explains to a Roman Catholic priest, "It isn't a question of agreeing with me—I have expressed no *opinion*. That is the *opinion* of the official Church, which you will find plainly stated in the Nicene Creed, whether or not you and I agree with it."[44] Dogma is the unchanging foundation—the orthodoxy—upon which the architecture of Christianity is solidly built, enabling it to accommodate renovations as culture changes.

Dogma versus Dogmatism—or Nott

Though encountering more than her fair share of heretical harangues from self-righteous Christians, Sayers wrote about the origin of the word *dogma*, quoted above, in response to an atheist: novelist and philosopher Kathleen Nott. In a 1953 book so popular it was republished in 1958, Nott attacked Sayers and C. S. Lewis, saying they were "braver and stupider than many of their orthodox literary fellows" due to their "tub-thumping" advocacy of Christianity. Asserting that Christian intellectuals like Lewis and Sayers were "engaged in the amputation and perversion of knowledge," Nott held up as the ideal source for truth the "open-minded inquiry" of science.[45]

Nott's sneering dismissal of Christianity illustrates how easily dogma—the opinions shared by a community, including an atheist community—can turn into dogmatism: the fanatical assertion of unquestioned assumptions about truth with no allowance for conversation about alternative viewpoints. Unfortunately, people like Nott tend to assume that assent to Christian dogma is inherently dogmatic while remaining oblivious to their own dogmatism. In contrast, Sayers knew the importance of distinguishing dogma from dogmatism. When a theologian alluded to her lack of dogmatism, she did not relish the compliment, mainly because he attributed Sayers's lack of dogmatism to a lack of dogma. In a letter of rebuttal written to *The Spectator*, Sayers states, "I cannot repudiate too strongly the suggestion that I have 'restated some of the Christian fundamentals . . . in terms more adapted to human needs than those of the ancient creed,' or that I have 'elaborated my own system of Christian teaching or doctrine.'"[46] She goes on to explain that her individualized language should never be understood as expressing a new belief better suited for contemporary society. As far as Sayers is concerned, the foundational doctrine of Christianity does not change; only the signs used to explain it change—in fact, *should* change—in order to avoid the idolatry of language. Clearly dismissing "the personal angle" to faith, Sayers instead promotes the shared opinion of the first four Ecumenical Councils, which established that Christ was fully human as well as fully God: a both/and paradigm. In contrast, dogmatists usually reduce knowledge to either/or categories: *either* you agree with my language about truth *or* you are a benighted fool.

Kathleen Nott clearly functioned according to either/or categories: either you stupidly promote Christianity or you intelligently acknowledge that only science leads to truth; either you superstitiously believe that God created humanity or you astutely recognize that life results from evolution; either you naïvely assert the Bible is inerrant or you acknowledge it is a human construction. Unfortunately, Christians often use the same either/or tactics: either you use King James English or you speak blasphemy; either you believe in free will or in God's election; either you emphatically support my political party or you have a flaccid faith. No wonder people are turning away from the church in droves; they see Christians operating not that much differently from people who revile Christianity, and the latter seeming to have a lot more fun (with an emphasis on *seeming*).

Christian Heresies: Then and Now

Committed to maintaining *both* ancient creeds *and* freedom of thought, Sayers recognized that Christian heresies often reflect either/or thought. In *The Emperor Constantine,* she focuses on the Arian heresy: the assertion by Arius and his followers that Christ was not both/and. Sayers thought long and hard about this problem, remarking in 1941, a full decade before *The Emperor Constantine,* that the Arian heresy was still alive and well, defining it in her own inimitable way: "there is somebody called God and a subsequent, inferior, but more sympathetic person called the Son of God, who had nothing to do with the creating the world, and whose part in running it is rather [like] that of a foreman of the works sadly put upon by the management."[47]

The Arian heresy continues to inform culture today; many people argue that one can follow Jesus without having to drag along all the supernatural baggage required by the Creeds. Responding to a correspondent baffled by Christian doctrine, Sayers asserts a distinction between believing Jesus was fully God and assuming Jesus was such a "perfect man" that God chose to "manifest" divinity through him: "It is the difference between pseudo-Christianity and Christianity," as she puts it. She then goes on explain that those who deny the both/and nature of Jesus are either non-Christian or Christian "Heretics of one school or another."[48] Sayers, here, is not attacking people who disagree with her; she is simply affirming the basic foundation of Christian orthodoxy and the original meaning of *heretic.* She parallels my father, who sought to protect the communally designed foundation of a hospital so that the building can accommodate future changes to its architecture. Significantly, the word *building* is *both* a noun *and* a verb. Like the noun/verb that names God, the "I am who I am" (Exodus 3:14), the building of Christianity is both a noun and a verb: an unchanging foundation that allows for change to the house of faith; a noun/verb grounded in the both/and of Jesus, the word of God.

Though disturbed by the either/or thought promoted by the Arian heresy, Sayers found far more annoying a Christian heresy at the other end of the spectrum: Docetism, which taught that Jesus, God on earth, was not *really* flesh. Its name based on a Greek root that means "to seem," Docetism held that Jesus only *seemed* to be human. And Sayers asserts that it was Docetists in her own day that caused the scandal over *The Man Born to Be King*. Christians horrified by the broadcasts reflected, in Sayers's words, "that Docetic and totally heretical Christology which denies the full Humanity of Our Lord."[49]

I can testify to something similar happening over half a century later. While early in my career as a college professor, I got in trouble with a parent of one of my Christian students because I mentioned, while teaching the poetry of Gerard Manley Hopkins, that Jesus was tempted by lust. Incensed, the parent called my department chair, demanding that the college fire me for such blasphemy, evidently unaware that I was alluding to a famous verse: "For we have not a high priest who is unable to sympathize with our weaknesses, but one who in every respect has been tempted as we are, yet without sinning" (Hebrews 4:15). Of course, I could have been doing what Arius did: quoting a Bible verse out of context to prove a point that I wanted to make. That is what Christians have done through the ages to support causes like slavery and the disenfranchisement of women. The verse to which I alluded, however, harmonizes with the opinion—dogma—established by the first four Ecumenical Councils. Because Jesus was *fully* human as well as *fully* God, he was tempted like any human—without giving in to temptation.

Sayers got into much more trouble than I did. Whereas I was accused of heresy only to my department chair, who knew enough about ancient dogma to deflect the demands of a Docetic mother, Sayers was accused of heresy in the pages of *Punch*, a national magazine. Ironically, this accusation was several years before *The Man Born to Be King* scandalized the country. Sayers was accused of using "free and easy theology" in *The Zeal of Thy House*, a play that merely mentions Christ's "temptations and suffering" rather than actually voicing them on the radio.[50] In a letter replying to *Punch*, Sayers despairs how Christians in the past as well as in her own day (not to mention my own day) have trouble accepting a fully human Jesus: a Jesus who sweats, who laughs, who eliminates digestive waste.

Sayers felt so troubled about Christian Docetism that she gave a radio talk called "The Sacrament of Matter" four months before *The Man Born to Be King* began its first broadcast. Listeners all over England heard her emphatically condemn "heretical" denunciations of the flesh:

> The Church does *not* say that matter is evil, nor that the body is evil. For her very life, she dare not. For her whole life is bound up in the doctrine that God Himself took human nature upon Him and went about this material world as a living man, with a human body and a human brain, and that he was perfect and sinless in the body as out of the body, in time as in eternity, in earth as in heaven. That is her creed; that is her dogma; that is the opinion to which she stands committed.[51]

Whereas the Docetic heresy implies matter is evil, the Arian heresy denies that Jesus was one substance with Creator God: opposite ends of the either/or spectrum. Sayers, in contrast, advocates both/and theology. As she tells the editor of *The Church*

Times, "To keep the exact middle course between Arianism and Docetism is always difficult, but one has to try and do it if one is not to lose the whole meaning for us of the Incarnation."[52]

Sayers advocates a "middle course" not merely for the sake of creedal conformism, however. She knows that the both/and of Christ's nature, encapsulated by the word *incarnation*, makes a radical difference for life as we live it. By taking on flesh, God fully understands our suffering, carrying to the grave consequences of self-serving behavior (i.e., sin) so that we don't have to. At the same time, God sanctified flesh through the incarnation, which should radically transform the way we view the human body and how it performs. Doctrine about the incarnation encourages us to confess our sin *and* to celebrate our embodiment; it is about both/and truth.

The Drama of Christianity

The "whole meaning" of the incarnation certainly transformed Sayers during her engagement with the Canterbury play—so much so that she felt led to compare the doctrinal foundation of Christianity with the stages upon which plays are performed. Writing "The Greatest Drama Ever Staged Is the Official Creed of Christendom" soon after *The Zeal of Thy House* opened in London, she wanted to communicate how "the most exciting drama that ever staggered the imagination of man" is the drama of God's murder, a drama that was staged in history, a drama based on fact. This "drama is summarized quite clearly in the Creeds of the Church, and if we think it dull, it is because we either have never really read those amazing documents, or have recited them so often and so mechanically as to have lost all sense of their meaning." The Creeds seem dull today for the same reason as in Sayers's era: Christians have turned Jesus into an unimaginative advocate for conserving the status quo. In contrast, as Sayers notes, "The people who hanged Christ never, to do them justice, accused Him of being a bore; on the contrary, they thought Him too dynamic to be safe."[53]

Many people considered Sayers too dynamic to be safe as well. Herself transformed by the subversive power of theater, Sayers knew that what makes drama exciting is change. Whereas movies stay exactly the same no matter when or where they are shown, live theater differs from performance to performance. This is due to the fact that, like Christian faith, theater is incarnational: the word on the page is made flesh on the stage. And, once flesh-and-blood bodies act on a stage, context affects what they do. As any stage actor will tell you, audiences can energize or deflate performances. Even the actions of fellow actors may change behavior on the stage, as when an actor trips or forgets lines from the script, causing others to make changes *in order to maintain the script* rather than abandon it.

Furthermore, even though the original script does not change, interpretations of the script change as culture changes. Think, for example, of new renditions of Shakespeare plays. Without changing his scripts, theater troupes perform the Bard's plays in ways that keep them relevant to our own time. Similarly, the script of ancient Christian doctrine does not change, but the way we perform that script does change. Like Christ himself, the performance is both/and: both preservation and transformation. This is why early Christian leaders decided to keep the Old Testament along with the New; the Bible preserves memory of God's work in the past while also proclaiming the radical transformation of

God's work through the incarnation. Perhaps not coincidentally, a second-century bishop who thought the Hebrew Bible (the Old Testament) should not be part of Christian Scripture also denounced the incarnation, arguing that it was "a disgrace" to conceive of God as fully flesh, since the human body is "stuffed with excrement."[54] As far as Bishop Marcion was concerned, both/and doctrine is outrageously subversive. His views were declared heretical as should be those of any Christian who prefers either/or thought.

How, then, might Christians apply both/and thought to the relationship between Christ and culture? How do we know when to defy and when to defer to cultural change? How do we follow the example of Christ who came not to destroy the law but to fulfill it? Seeking to seriously grapple with these questions, Sayers challenged the status quo not for the sake of innovation as an end in itself, but *in order to maintain the script* of Christian orthodoxy, composed between 325 and 451 CE at the first four Ecumenical Councils. She considered as her model Jesus Christ, who, as she puts it, "always encouraged people to ask questions about Him, and never minded how ignorant or even how wicked they were, so long as they really wanted to know and weren't just trying to show off and be superior. And what he said about Himself was that He was one with God."[55]

Following the subversive example of Christ is not for the faint of heart. Like Tyndale, who was burned at the stake for questioning church teachings after translating Scripture into English; like Luther, who was excommunicated for defying centuries-old interpretations of Christian truth; like Galileo, who was imprisoned by church leaders for proclaiming that the earth moved around the sun, Sayers was excoriated by Christians resistant to escalator-like movement. Nevertheless, Sayers wants us to join her on the escalator, knowing that, while "yet it moves," it is fixed to a firm foundation.

Not coincidentally, "and yet it moves" is the line Galileo reputedly uttered about the earth's orbit following his trial before church inquisitors. We should not be surprised, then, that Sayers quotes Galileo's Italian, *eppur si muove* [and yet it moves], in a letter about her own subversive writings. Significantly, the letter was to another subversive Christian: C. S. Lewis, whose work, like an escalator, has moved thousands up and beyond in their faith.[56]

CHAPTER TWO
RELIGIOUS SHOPPING AND EXCHANGE

Sayers risked queasiness on a store's "moving staircase" because she liked to shop. She died, in fact, immediately after shopping for Christmas gifts, falling at the bottom of her stationary staircase soon after returning home. During World War II, however, she willingly refrained from shopping in order to serve her country, worried that British citizens would regress into habits of mindless consumerism after the war. Sayers understood how easy it is to be "bamboozled by our vanity, indolence, and greed into keeping the squirrel cage of wasteful economy turning."[1] And she knew better than most what kept the wheel inside the cage sufficiently oiled: advertising.

While writing her early detective novels, Sayers supported herself by working for a London advertising firm. Contributing to some of the most effective advertising campaigns of the 1920s—for Guinness beer and Colman's mustard—Sayers reputedly coined the phrase "it pays to advertise," if even cynically.[2] Composing ad copy for nearly a decade had alerted her to the narcotic effects of advertising and the consumer addictions it feeds. In her ninth novel, *Murder Must Advertise* (1933), Sayers connects advertising with narcotics quite literally, inventing a character that creates codes out of newspaper ads to signal distribution sites for illegal drugs. In fact, she has Wimsey's brother-in-law, Chief Inspector Charles Parker, state, "As far as I can make out, all advertisers are dope-merchants."[3] Indeed, when Lord Peter goes undercover at an advertising agency to solve a murder, he encounters a mystery far more baffling than the crime he was called to investigate:

> If all the advertising in the world were to shut down tomorrow, would people still go on buying more soap, eating more apples, giving their children more vitamins, . . . re-decorating their houses, refreshing themselves with more non-alcoholic thirst-quenchers, cooking more new, appetizing dishes, affording themselves that little extra touch which means so much? Or would the whole desperate whirligig slow down, and the exhausted public relapse upon plain grub and elbow-grease? He did not know.[4]

Though Lord Peter uncovers the murderer and exposes the narcotics ring, he fails to answer these questions, which are just as relevant today as when Sayers wrote them. Consumers, "aching for a luxury beyond their reach and for a leisure for ever [sic] denied them," are easily "bullied or wheedled into spending their few hardly won shillings on whatever might give them, if only for a moment, a leisured and luxurious illusion."[5]

Several years later, Sayers explicitly denounces "the furious barrage of advertisement by which people are flattered and frightened out of a reasonable contentment into a greedy hankering after goods which they do not really need."[6] Sayers wrote these words in an essay on the seven deadly sins, seeking to warn Christians against the sin of "gluttonous consumption."[7]

Consumer Addictions

Fueled by advertising, gluttonous consumption is still alive and well among Christians. During a Bible study on the West Coast, I was dismayed when a woman, bemoaning California real estate prices, echoed advertising slogans by proclaiming, in all seriousness, "I have a right to own a house with hardwood floors." On the East Coast a decade later, I overheard a Christian tell her husband, "I feel drained and useless; I need to go shopping." Rather than fellowshipping to alleviate dissatisfaction with life, it's much easier to go fellow-shopping, seeking transformation through buying something—anything.

In Sayers's day as well as our own, people tend to get more satisfaction from buying goods than from doing good, such that "wor-shopping" has replaced worshipping—a pun not as far-fetched as it may sound. The *wor* in *worship* is derived from the term *worth*; it's all about the worth of the good(s). Anyone who considers such wordplay irreverent should take note of one of the most ironic etymologies in the English language: the relationship between *mercenary* and *mercy*. Like many terms having to do with shopping—mercantile, merchant, market, and merchandise— *mercenary* and *mercy* derive from a Latin root meaning "goods." All the words except *mercy*, of course, allude to goods received through exchange: you give money at the market, merchants give merchandise in exchange; you supply mercenaries with money, they fight your wars in exchange. *Mercy* is the only word in the list that grants the good(s) without any transaction fee. *Mercy*, in other words, is a gift.

Grateful for God's unmerited mercy, Dorothy Sayers worried that people seem to value merchandise more than mercy, preferring goods to the Good. She was especially outraged by our addictive tendency to assess the worth of people in terms of how much money they make: "Has the fact that enthusiastic crowds cheer and scream around professional footballers, while offering no enthusiastic greeting to longshoremen, anything to do with the wages offered to footballers and longshoremen respectively?"[8] Her concern helps explain the hesitancy she wrote into the character of Harriet Vane, who repeatedly declined Lord Peter's marriage proposals. Enjoying her financial independence as a successful author, she wasn't sure she wanted to marry an aristocrat born into wealth and privilege, a man used to getting whatever he wanted. To make things worse, Harriet owed Peter her life; marriage to him felt like a form of exchange, destabilizing the possibility of love as a gift.

In real life, people like Harriet, and Sayers who created her, seem to be exceptions to the rule. I had an unimpressive college student once tell me, "Girls like to go out with me because I drive a Jaguar." His shallow comment reflects a disturbing cultural norm, wherein inarticulate, untalented, and self-serving persons get national attention and leadership positions primarily because they are rich. Their goods speak louder than any signs of goodness, their selfish behavior excused because they have money and hence cultural power. But there was something that disturbed Sayers much more: a consumerist model for Christianity itself. She recognized that even the most earnest of believers often define their faith according to an "economy of exchange."

The Relativism of Exchangism

The phrase *economy of exchange*, along with the coinage *exchangism*, was used by philosopher Jacques Derrida to explain how people conceptualize the way language works. Similar to giving a coin in exchange for a product while shopping, you give a word in exchange for a concept, as when you say "MOVE!" to someone blocking an escalator. More complex statements, of course, necessitate many more words, just as more expensive items demand many more coins. Exchange is fundamental to all human societies, both linguistically and sociologically, even when coins are not involved. Unlike other animals, we thrive on exchange.

Because exchange is so basic to being human, it starts influencing how we think about religion. Just as different countries use different forms of currency—pesos in Mexico, pennies in America, pence in England—various religions use different words for the concept of God. This difference leads to equal and opposite problems that troubled Sayers. First, religious people develop a tendency to assume that only certain words can be exchanged for truth about God, evidenced by the scandal Sayers generated when her BBC radio plays didn't use King James English; Christians thought she was using counterfeit coin.[9]

Equally simplistic for Sayers is the opposite extreme: the belief that *any* language works to capture the truth because all religions lead to the same God. Worshipping thus becomes reduced to another kind of wor-shopping. Like shoppers who can purchase effective laundry detergent whether exchanging money for Wisk or for Tide, seekers can find the same God no matter what religion they buy (into). Though Sayers acknowledges that "other religions have caught glimpses of the truth," she refuses a relativistic approach to faith wherein "all religions are equally good," as she puts it.[10] Instead, she would emphatically agree with famous post-modern philosopher Richard Rorty who states that, "'Relativism' is the view that every belief on a certain topic, or perhaps about any topic, is as good as any other. No one holds this view."[11] By "no one," Rorty means no careful and critical thinker—like Dorothy L. Sayers.

As far as Sayers was concerned, people who argue that all religions worship the same God are suggesting they have a God-like ability to transcend language, implying that they know the truth because they can float above dogma: the differing *opinions* about God that are delineated in language. Richard Rorty challenges such naïveté, writing that "speaking a language . . . is not a trait a man can lose while retaining the power of thought. So there is no chance that someone can take up a vantage point for comparing conceptual schemes by temporarily shedding his own."[12] Human understanding of God is always embedded in language, and because different religions speak about divinity in different ways, they do not worship the same God.

Nevertheless, as Sayers explains to one Anglican priest, "Christians have too weakly acquiesced in a vague religiosity and the worship of nothing-in-particular. We have been so anxious to avoid the charge of dogmatism and heresy-hunting that we have rather lost sight of the idea that Christianity is supposed to be an interpretation of the universe."[13] Some may think Sayers's word "interpretation" throws Christianity back into the stew of relativism, as though to say, "Whereas I interpret God this way, you interpret God that way, but the same God allows us to cook up recipes in different savory sauces." But she does not encourage such assumptions to enter her theological kitchen.

Having thought long and hard about relativism, Sayers suggested that its rise after World War I paved the way for Hitler. British leaders, wanting to avoid a second world war at all costs, preached tolerance, suggesting that it didn't matter if Germans buy Wisk and the British Tide, because both are committed to clean living. As Sayers less fancifully put it in 1943, "We said that it was just that people had 'different ideas'—ideas didn't matter—all truth was relative—good and evil were just names for different points of view."[14] Hitler's rise to power demonstrated not only that ideas matter, but also how they can become invested with religious significance very quickly. In a speech delivered during the war, Sayers says of the Nazis:

> The immense spiritual strength of our opponents lies precisely in the fact that they have fervently embraced, and hold with fanatical fervor, a dogma which is nonetheless a dogma for being called an "ideology." . . . The rulers of Germany have seen quite clearly that dogma and ethics are inextricably bound together. . . . It is only with great difficulty that we can bring ourselves to grasp the fact that there is no failure in Germany to live up to her own standards of right conduct. It is something much more terrifying and tremendous: it is that what we believe to be evil, Germany believes to be good.[15]

The Nazi dogma of Aryan supremacy proves, for Sayers, that "It is a lie to say that dogma does not matter; it matters enormously."[16] German Christians caught up in religious fervor for the Fuehrer had supplanted ancient dogma about Christ's sacrifice for the entire world with political dogmatism: a problem that has marred and scarred Christianity throughout the ages.

Some skeptics, in fact, have pointed to Hitler-cheering Christians to argue that, rather than equally good, all religions are equally bad, perpetuating cruelty in some form or another. Sayers would respond by asking them to explain from where they got their sense of cruelty in the first place. As she noted a bit later during the war, "even the most anti-religious of our thinkers" believe that "fully enlightened humanity" are not "cruel." And then she asks "But why? What makes us so sure about this?" For her, atheists who revile Hitler are hard pressed to explain the basis upon which they determine universal values of good versus evil. After all, Hitler promoted, as do many atheists, a vigorous utilitarian ethic: the greatest good for the greatest number. The fact that atheists were horrified by Hitler's definition of the "good" and his Aryan assessment of "the greatest number" illustrates Sayers's point: "at the very basis of our thought and behaviour there lies a pair of assumptions which are wholly religious—which reason cannot prove and for which science can offer no evidence. We assume that both our conception of the good and our human reason are really valid."[17] She would once again ask where these assumptions come from. To be intellectually consistent, those who believe there is no God, and hence no universal standard of good and evil, can only answer with "Hitler offends *my culture's* definition of goodness." It is as though to say, "Whereas my community believes Wisk is superior, Hitler's community chose Tide instead, which it used for ethnic cleansing."

The Cleansing of Relativism

Sayers firmly believed that Christian dogma subverts such problematic relativism. In a BBC radio talk delivered during the war, she acknowledges that most people think "Jesus was a nicer sort of man than Hitler." She follows up this cheeky understatement with an even more subversive suggestion: we have no "assurance" that the world will "get on better" by following Jesus rather than Hitler if, as non-Christians assert, Jesus was a human like the rest of us. If he died, as is the fate of all humans, Jesus is no longer "in a position to make His influence very actively felt." And then Sayers throws the knock-down punch: "But if Jesus Christ is God of God, and made the world to His own pattern, then the situation is very different; for in that case, by disregarding Christ we shall come into collision with the very nature of the universe."[18] Sayers, in other words, believed that Christian dogma explains the nature of the universe better than any other religion. Created by a loving God, it is one in which genocide is abhorrent.

Many people will react, quite understandably, with frustration: "How, then, could God have allowed the Holocaust to happen?" Ever subversive, Sayers would respond with an outrageously counterintuitive answer: evil happens because God is good. Rather than creating marionettes with strings that can be pulled to control behavior, God endowed humans with the goodness of freedom, enabling them to freely choose either to embrace goodness or to pursue their own selfish interests, which is the source of all evil. That's not relativism; it's revelation: the revelation of a universe that operates according to God's endorsement of free will as a human good. People across all spectrums of belief will agree that freedom is an inherent good that turns evil when used to violate the freedoms of innocent others.

Genocide, of course, should make our hearts ache to the point of despair, reducing tidy theological explanations to callow insensitivity. Sayers subversively turns the table by suggesting it is equally callow to *use* knowledge about the Holocaust to support our own interests: either as a justification to renounce belief in God or as an excuse not to think about our own evil choices. As Hitler's self-aggrandizing purposes became more glaring in the spring of 1938, Sayers wrote an article for the *Sunday Times* that addresses this issue:

> "Why doesn't God smite this dictator dead?" is a question a little remote from us. Why, madam, did He not strike you dumb and imbecile before you uttered that baseless and unkind slander the day before yesterday? . . . And why, sir, did He not cause your hand to rot off at the wrist before you signed your name to that dirty little bit of financial trickery? . . . Your misdeeds and mine are nonetheless repellent because our opportunities for doing damage are less spectacular than those of some other people.[19]

Sayers follows up with two summarizing questions: "Why did God create his universe on these lines at all? Why did He not make us mere puppets, incapable of executing anything but His own pattern of perfection?" Her answer is that love can be true only when freely offered. God, who is love, therefore gave humans total freedom to either love their Creator or to turn their backs on God in order to blindly serve their own self-interests.

As far as Sayers was concerned, Christianity is far more subversive than atheism in its emphasis on the goodness of freedom and the sacrificial nature of genuine love. Ancient dogma established that, even though humans chose self-interest over seeking the Source of all love, God, as Sayers puts it, "loved His own creation so completely that He became part of it, suffered with and for it, and made it a sharer in His own glory and fellow worker with Himself in the working out of His own design for it."[20]

Sayers's references to "sharer" and "fellow worker" are important. God is not a Transcendent Boss that expects underlings to do certain tasks in order to earn their due reward. True love, in other words, renounces an economy of exchange. Even the most hardened atheist recognizes a lack of love in anyone who says, "I'll love you *only if* you do something for me in exchange." The God of Christianity renounces exchangism, preferring to be in relationship with all of creation, such that each and every human can be a "sharer" and "fellow worker" in that creation.

Christian Exchangism

Defying religious relativism and the economy of exchange that fuels it, Sayers found it quite ironic that many Christians, though vociferously denouncing relativism, make their faith seem very similar to other religions through an implicit, sometimes downright explicit, endorsement of exchangism.

Assuming that bad things happen because people have displeased the gods, exchangist religions teach that one must appease transcendent powers through prescribed rituals or good works, thus exchanging good actions for blessings from above. In contrast, Christian dogma subversively asserts that followers of Christ don't pay the price of salvation; God does. Christianity is not based upon exchangist transactions, lest anyone should boast. As Sayers succinctly puts it, "the perfection of God's act doesn't depend on us."[21] She felt strongly about this issue perhaps because an economy of exchange had warped her understanding of Christianity for decades.

Born to a father who served as a rector in the Anglican Church, Sayers internalized a sacramental approach to faith that beautifully captures a basic Christian truth: because God endorsed flesh through the incarnation, we express gratitude for salvation through Christ by way of our own flesh. High Church Anglicans like Sayers therefore practice, in the flesh, the traditional sacraments of Roman Catholicism, considering Baptism and Eucharist imperative, while encouraging Confirmation, Ordination, Confession, Holy Matrimony, and Anointing of the Sick. Sayers even inherited the embodied practice of crossing herself before meals, a response that she maintained into adulthood.

Though they profoundly reflect the embodiment essential to Christian orthodoxy, focus on the sacraments can easily fall into exchangism. I knew someone who described his attraction to sacramental Christianity in such terms: "It's great, because I can sin all I want during the week and it's all erased by Confession and Eucharist on Sunday." Though he was sincere, his attitude differed little from a go-through-these-rites-and-you-appease-the-gods religion. A similar kind of exchangism helps explain Sayers's response to the sacrament of Confirmation during her boarding school days. Writing home shortly after being confirmed in Salisbury Cathedral, the adolescent Dorothy described the service to her parents as "awfully nice" and "beautifully arranged."[22] But decades later she regarded her Confirmation as a distasteful task she felt compelled to undergo, a requirement that generated "resentment against religion in general which lasted a long time."[23] One biographer suggests Sayers's earlier response is most authentic, whereas another believes the later statement more accurately captures Sayers's perception.[24] But perhaps both responses are valid. As a youth she was excited for the event because she perceived it as a necessary step in Christianity's economy of exchange: fulfill this rite and you please God (and your parents). This may partially explain why the young Sayers, though never abandoning her faith, tended to marginalize it. Because she periodically inserted sacramental coins into the church meter, she could park her thoughts wherever she wanted. But by her mid-thirties she felt manipulated by such requirements, resenting the exchangism of "religion in general."

Writing to an Anglican priest not long after *The Zeal of Thy House* changed her life, Sayers despairs that "there is a deeply-rooted conviction in most people's minds that Sacraments are magic."[25] Sayers clearly critiques "people's minds" rather than the sacraments, echoing Protestant reformer John Calvin, who denounced "the error of a magical conception of the sacraments." In his *Institutes of the Christian Religion* (1536), Calvin goes on to critique superstitious assumptions even about the language a priest uses during the sacrament of Eucharist, as though the Biblical words about Christ's body and blood were a "magical incantation."[26] By the next century, Protestants were suggesting that a term associated with magic, *hocus pocus*, was a corruption of *Hoc est Corpus* ("This is the Body") spoken by priests during Latin Eucharist. Language about Christ's sacrifice, *Hoc est Corpus*, had degenerated for many people into *hocus pocus*: a magical coin of exchange.

Convinced that the problem was with "people's minds," Sayers did not abandon sacramental Christianity for a more evangelical approach to faith. In her letters, she almost always uses the word *evangelical* with dismay. She apparently recognized in evangelicalism an economy of exchange more problematic than that of the Anglicanism she shared with C. S. Lewis.

Sayers and Evangelical Faith

In his stellar work *Evangelicalism in Modern Britain: A History from the 1730s to the 1980s*, David W. Bebbington identifies four primary emphases in evangelical Christianity.[27] To make them easier to remember, I think of them as the ABCC's of evangelicals:

A for Activism: the need to actively address the world's needs

B for Biblicism: all essential truth about faith is contained in the Bible

C for Crucifixion: salvation is made possible through Christ's death on the cross

C for Conversion: authentic faith results from a conversion experience

As with sacramental Christianity, these profound strengths can have accompanying weaknesses, due to the exchangism ingrained in "people's minds." Sayers found several things troubling about evangelicalism: 1) an emphasis on emotionalism; 2) the celebration of dramatic conversion experiences; 3) the burden to evangelize and convert others; 4) a "bibliolatry" similar to that which caused the *Man Born to Be King* controversy. These weaknesses, for her, become most problematic when laced with a consumerism that emphasizes blessings gained in exchange for faith.

To her credit, Sayers quite readily admits that she has a prejudice against emotional worship experiences, due to the fact that she cannot at all relate to them. As she once explained to C. S. Lewis, "All spiritual experience is a closed book to me; in that respect I have been tone-deaf from birth." She endorses the Creeds, she tells him, not because they bring comfort or exhilaration but because they appeal to her "imaginative intellect," making sense of God's desire to free humans from the bondage of sin.[28] Acknowledging that emotionally uplifting experiences are important for many Christians, she nevertheless argues that they are not *necessary* for passionate faith.

For Sayers, and Christians like her, passion takes another form. When someone challenged her to be more forthright in sharing her faith journey—to give her testimony, as evangelicals might put it—Sayers wrote a long letter asserting that she can identify no moment of conversion, having believed in Christ's death and resurrection her whole life: "I am quite without the thing known as 'inner light' or 'spiritual experience.' I have never undergone conversion. . . . I cannot go to people and say: 'I know the movements of the spirit from within.'" Once again asserting that she is "quite incapable of 'religious emotion,'" she proceeds to identify her attraction to Christianity as intellectual, this time talking about her "passionate intellect": an intellect that loves the way Christian doctrine can explain not only the existence of good and evil, but also God's sacrificial love for humanity.[29] Furthermore, and more importantly, due to its explanatory power, which includes resistance to an economy of exchange, she believes Christian dogma to be true.

This, however, did not generate any evangelistic zeal in Sayers. Numerous times throughout her letters, Sayers says that she is not an evangelist, despite the fact that she helped ignite or reignite the faith of thousands. For her, the concept that God calls all Christians to evangelize ignores Scripture as well as church dogma. After all, Paul emphasizes to both the Corinthians (1 Corinthians 12:1–31) and the Romans (12:4–10) that the church is made of members with diverse gifts, only one of which, as Paul tells the Ephesians, is evangelism (4:11). Instead of the gift of evangelism, Sayers believes God granted her the gift of teaching: educating people in the intellectual integrity of ancient doctrine and its applicability to contemporary society. As she explains to the editor of the *Catholic Herald*, "I haven't got a pastoral mind or a passion to convert people; but I hate having my intellect outraged by imbecile ignorance and by the monstrous distortions of fact which the average heathen accepts as being 'Christianity' (and from which he most naturally revolts)."[30] Sayers therefore delivers lectures and radio talks, composes newspaper and magazine articles, writes books and plays: all to educate people about the facts of Christian doctrine. Though her goal is not to evangelize, she ends up drawing people to faith by appealing to their intellects, not to their emotions.

In addition to the gift of teaching, some would suggest that Sayers had the gift of prophesy, due to the brilliant way she subverted "monstrous distortions" in Christianity. The director of religious programming at the BBC wrote Sayers to say, "We must make you a prophet to this generation and hand you the microphone to use as often as you feel able." Convinced that this was not her gift, Sayers told an assistant director at the BBC, "I am not a prophet, but only a sort of painstaking explainer of official dogma."[31] Committed to thinking well more than feeling good, Sayers encourages believers and unbelievers alike to get the facts straight about Christian dogma:

> It is fatal to let people suppose that Christianity is only a mode of feeling; it is vitally necessary to insist that it is first and foremost a rational explanation of the universe. It is hopeless to offer Christianity as a vaguely idealistic aspiration of a simple and consoling kind; it is, on the contrary, a hard, tough, exacting, and complex doctrine, steeped in a drastic and uncompromising realism.[32]

This emphasis upon intelligent understanding of the Creeds reveals another reason Sayers resisted evangelical emphasis on the emotional uplift of feel-good spirituality. She recognized that a focus on feelings can easily reinforce an economy of exchange: if you accept Jesus into your heart and worship him with zeal, you will receive comforting blessings *in return*. As she put it in 1941, when the London Blitz had driven many people to take sudden interest in Christianity, "one has a haunting feeling that God's acquaintance is being cultivated because He might come in useful. But God is quite shrewd enough to see through that particular kind of commercial fraud."[33] Employing an economic metaphor, Sayers knew that exchangism runs counter to what distinguishes Christianity from other religions. Hence, Christians who buy into an economy of exchange engage in what she calls "blasphemous hypocrisy, which ends by degrading God to the status of a heathen fetish, bound to the service of a tribe, and liable to be dumped head downward in the water butt if He failed to produce good harvest weather in return for services rendered."[34]

Working for Evangelical Blessings

Part of the problem may go back to "the Protestant work ethic," a phrase made famous by Max Weber, a German sociologist contemporary with Sayers's parents.[35] Sayers aligns the Protestant work ethic with exchangism in a speech she delivered during World War II:

> "Work hard and be thrifty, and God will bless you with a contented mind and [financial] competence." This is nothing but enlightened self-interest in its vulgarest form, and plays directly into the hands of the monopolist and the financier. Nothing has so deeply discredited the Christian Church as Her squalid submission to the economic theory of society.[36]

Sayers would be discouraged (though not surprised) to discover that an economy of exchange continues to rule the way many evangelicals approach their faith, as testified to by *Christianity Today*, one of the most respected evangelical journals in the world. Its November 2018 issue reports a LifeWay Research survey in which 41 percent of "Americans with evangelical beliefs" say that "their church 'teaches that if I give more money to my church and charities, God will bless me *in return*.'" The next month, the magazine reported another LifeWay survey question in which 32 percent of American evangelicals agreed that "God will always reward faith with material blessings."[37]

These findings dovetail with the prosperity theology of the so-called "Health and Wealth Gospel." Ross Douthat, a Roman Catholic columnist for the *New York Times,* aligns prosperity theology with "name it and claim it" Christianity, which teaches that job promotions, family successes, and financial blessings signal "divine providence responding to your petitions, and holding up heaven's end of *the bargain* Jesus made." There is, of course, a negative side to such exchangism: if you "fall into struggles and suffering it's a sign that you just haven't prayed hard enough, or trusted faithfully enough, or thought big enough, or otherwise behaved the way a child of God really should."[38] Sayers would emphatically endorse the title Douthat gave his 2012 book: *Bad Religion*.

The subversive Sayers, in fact, anticipated Douthat's critique by eighty years. In "Thought for the Day," written for BBC radio around 1940, she talks about Christians who blithely quote the verse about "faith as a grain of mustard-seed" (Luke 17:6) while telling others in crisis that *if* they had believed more, *if* they had prayed more, *then* they would have experienced a miracle.

Punning on the mustard-seed reference, Sayers calls such exchangism "a seedy condition" of faith:

> There is something sordid in that kind of heavenly book-keeping which shows a payment of a quid of miracle against a quo of faith; & it is very doubtful whether the Lord of the Vineyard balances his books on that principle. I am reminded of another indignant letter in another paper, discussing the case of a lame man who had made the pilgrimage to Lourdes & not been healed. "The man," said this correspondent, "had a right to expect a miracle." God had, so to speak, taken his money on false pretences.[39]

Notice how Sayers explicitly aligns such "seedy" faith with financial exchange. She knew that, when Christians think according to principles of "Health and Wealth," their reason for worshipping differs little from wor-shopping: a matter of shopping around for the religion that delivers the best exchange rate.

And she clearly knew that many do the same thing with the Bible, shopping around for passages that support what they want to believe anyway. While genuine worshippers ask the Holy Spirit to reveal truth through their Bible reading, wor-shoppers pick and choose verses that fit their worldview, much as they pick and choose trousers that fit their bodies. Such wor-shopping bothered Sayers even in her youth, making her all the more hesitant to openly proclaim her Christian faith. In her very first novel (*Whose Body?*, 1923), she includes an exchange between Lord Peter Wimsey and his friend Detective Inspector Parker, who is reading a commentary on the Epistle to the Galatians. Lord Peter states of biblical interpreters, "All these men work with a bias in their minds; one way or other . . . they find what they are looking for."[40]

This is how wor-shoppers endorse prosperity theology. They comb Scripture until they find what they are looking for: verses that confirm their bias toward an exchangist God.

Sayers would not be surprised that scholars have paralleled prosperity theology with the medieval buying and selling of indulgences that guaranteed easier passage through purgatory: the economy of exchange that motivated Martin Luther to nail ninety-five theses to the Wittenberg door about problematic Christian practices. Wanting to counteract the demise of Christianity into one among many exchangist religions, Luther energetically preached salvation by "grace alone."[41]

Salvation by Grace Alone

Sayers shared Luther's commitment to grace alone, which, as far as she was concerned, sent Christians back to the subversive truth of the earliest church Creeds. After composing her fifth *Man Born to Be King* radio play, which contains Christ's Sermon on the Mount, she wrote to the director of religious broadcasting to explain, "I have translated and glossed the Beatitudes rather freely. I wanted to get rid of the 'reward and punishment' notion that has got attached to them."[42] As she realized, reward and punishment thinking perpetuates primitive religious impulses. In contrast, the apostle Paul states, in a letter that inspired leaders at the Ecumenical Councils, "For by grace you have been saved through faith; and this is not your own doing, it is the gift of God—not the result of works, so that no one may boast" (Ephesians 2:8–9). Sayers puts this truth into the mouth of Christ in her 1946 play *The Just Vengeance*. After stating that the law functions according to "bare merit"—an economy of exchange—Jesus proclaims that the loving "gifts" extended by God are gifts indeed: "beyond desert, beyond desire."[43] The Gospel message, like salvation itself, is offered in love: a subversive idea that many Christians profess but do not practice.

This may be due to the fact that even gift-giving in our culture operates by an economy of exchange. Think of the commonly asked question "will we be *exchanging* gifts?" or of the many stores that advertise "Free Gift with Purchase," an oxymoron if there ever was one. Sayers identified such oxymoronic exchangism with Father Christmas, or Santa Claus, who provides "gifts" *in exchange for* good behavior. As children grow up, they therefore treat God like a transcendent Santa Claus, praying for things they want, much as they once asked their local mall Santa for toys. When bad things happen, as Sayers bemoans, they therefore "cry aloud to the Father-Christmas-God who was the only God they had ever heard of." But then she follows up with shock of the old: "God was not in the nursery, handing out presents to good boys—He was on the cross beside them."[44]

This, then, is the gift of salvation, based not on works— whether works of charity, sacrament, or language—but on the murder of God: a murder redeemed by Christ's resurrection from the dead. Because of this act, we are offered the gift of forgiveness. Ironically, many Christians so emphasize the importance of believing this profound truth that they reduce belief itself to an economy of exchange, as though to say, "you must offer God this coin of belief in order to get salvation in return."

Sayers recognized that belief was essential to Christian faith. But it comes into play only insofar as we cannot *accept* a gift unless we *believe* one has been offered. Nothing *we* do can earn us salvation from the corruption of sin. It is Jesus who saves us, not our belief, no matter the exchange rate. Sayers, in fact, reputedly responded to a person's query "When were you saved?" with the cheeky, though profoundly orthodox, reply, "When Christ rose from the dead!" In contrast to the evangelical emphasis on dramatic conversion experiences, she maintained that salvation is freely offered by Christ, not the result of shopping for the best gift with purchase.

Shopping for the Savior

Sayers inserts shopping into her controversial radio plays about Jesus, not only to show biblical characters participating in activities her listeners understood, but also as a way to grapple with the radical difference between an economy of exchange and the gift of salvation. Her fourth play, *The Heirs to the Kingdom* (not *The Buyers of the Kingdom*) begins with a scene in which Philip discovers he was short-changed at the marketplace while purchasing food for the disciples. Simon (not yet renamed Peter) expresses his frustration with Philip's economic naïveté: "But here's me and Andrew and the Zebedees working all night with the nets to get a living for the lot of us—and then you go and let yourself be swindled by the first cheating salesman you meet in the bazaar."[45]

Like many of the fictional interactions in her plays, Sayers invents this relatable experience to contextualize the teachings of Jesus. In this instance, Philip's experience while shopping provides the backdrop for Christ's parable of the unrighteous steward (Luke 16:1–13), in which Jesus tells His disciples, "Learn how to deal with the world and make friends with worldly people, so that when everything earthly fails you may know the way to their hearts. . . . If you can't handle the goods of this world, how can you be trusted to handle the true treasures of Heaven?"[46] This exhortation explains why Sayers wrote the radio plays the way she did, using worldly language and situations to change the way people think about Christianity. And one of the things she wanted to change was the idea that access to the treasures of heaven depends upon an economy of exchange.

Sayers makes this very clear through her dramatization of the thieves on either side of the crucified Christ. Using the names given in the apocryphal Gospel of Nicodemus, which dates back to the fourth century, Sayers gives Gestas a humorously snarky personality while Dysmas, the penitent thief, exhibits tender empathy. But then she does something tremendously subversive. She shows that Dysmas's famous words to Christ, reported only by Luke (23:42), were said *not in belief* that it was God on the cross beside him, but because he felt sorry for this "looney" Jesus who *thinks* "he's Goddamighty."[47]

To emphasize her point, Sayers includes a direction for the actor voicing the famous statement of Dysmas: "(*In a deeply respectful tone, humoring this harmless lunacy*) Sir, you'll remember me, won't you, when you come into your kingdom?" It is only when Jesus responds "I tell you—to-day you shall be with me in Paradise" that Dysmas realizes Jesus truly *is* God Almighty: "(*after an astonished pause and in a changed tone*) You're not mad!" And Dysmas proceeds to humbly confess his unworthiness.[48] In other words, Dysmas was saved *not by his belief* but by Jesus, who offered him a gift (the treasures of Paradise) that Dysmas accepted. Like Dysmas changing his tone, Sayers changed the entire tone of a traditional scene to shock us out of our reduction of Christianity to an economy of exchange. And she makes clear that this was her intent from the very start.

Supplanting Exchangism with the Gift

The first play Sayers wrote for *The Man Born to Be King* deals with the Slaughter of the Innocents, the incident when Herod arranges to kill all babies under the age of two after the Magi tell him of a newly born king (Matthew 2:1-18). Sayers, however, adds an extra motivation for Herod's slaughter: a detail included in Josephus's history of the Jews, written around 93 or 94 CE. Josephus tells of a riot in which Jews tear down the Roman Eagle insignia that Herod had placed on the Jewish Temple. Having read Josephus, Sayers adds a scene after the three Magi present gifts to the baby Jesus, a scene in which Herod watches as rioting Jews denounce the Eagle as an "odious symbol of a pagan power." Immediately afterward, she has Herod receive a note from the Magi saying that they must break their promise of seeing him after finding the baby to which the star is pointing. Herod psychologically connects their refusal to identify the newborn they worshipped with the Jewish riot: "It means trouble. Worse trouble. Insurrection. Civil war."[49] He therefore orders the slaughter of babies not only out of fear that Jews will set up one of those newborns as king, but also *in exchange for* their riot.

Like the gifts of the Magi, the slaughter of the innocents appears in no Gospel other than Matthew. Perhaps, as a former tax collector, Matthew was especially sensitive to economies of exchange. This would explain the Gospel writer's contrast between Herod, who selfishly thinks only of his own power and status, and the Magi, who, expecting nothing in exchange, offer gifts in gratitude for God's gift, born in a manger. Later in *The Man Born to Be King*, Sayers proves this is precisely what she had in mind.

In her eleventh play, Sayers invents a detail whereby one of the Magi returns to Jerusalem, arriving just as the man born to be king is taken down from the cross. Using a traditional Magi name that dates back to a Greek manuscript from around 500 CE, she has Mary address the returning Balthazar while cradling her crucified son in her arms: "I know you, King Balthazar. These are the baby hands that closed upon your gift of myrrh."[50] Magi gifts foreshadow Jesus as God's gift to the world: a gift not based on exchange, lest anyone should boast. Indeed, in her notes to the play, Sayers explicitly states that she inserts Balthazar into the crucifixion scene in order to connect it with the first play. We must pay attention, then, when she has Balthazar tell the other Magi in that first script, "I looked at the Child. And all about him lay the shadow of death, and all within him was the light of life; and I knew that I stood in the presence of the Mortal-Immortal, which is last secret of the universe."[51] Furthermore, by placing Balthazar in both plays, Sayers implies another parallel: like Herod the Great, who endorsed the slaughter of innocent babies in exchange for defying political power, Herod Antipas, his son, endorsed the slaughter of innocent Jesus in exchange for defying religious power.

In between these two famous murders by two self-serving Herods, Sayers repeatedly focuses on the difference between gift and exchange. For example, she emphasizes the juxtaposition of Christ's first miracle—the unearned, totally extravagant gift of turning water into wine—with Christ's whipping the money changers out of the Temple (John 2:1–17). Seeing a place of worship reduced to a mall for the buying and selling of sacrifices, Jesus demonstrates the outrage we all should feel toward wor-shopping. Sayers foreshadows this economy of exchange by placing a reference to exchangism in the Cana wedding scene that precedes it. After Jesus turns water into wine, characters express amazement that Jesus did not "pronounce any magical words"—like *abra-cadabra* or *hocus pocus*—in exchange for His miracle.[52] She thus emphasizes that the miracle was a pure gift, anticipating the pure gift of Christ's sacrifice on the cross.

Sayers even shows Jesus having to pry his disciples away from exchangist thought. When John sincerely remarks, "Feed God's people, and they will praise His name," she has Simon agree: "Yes, we are taught to love God for His mercies." Jesus, however, counters that they are to love God "for Himself first . . . *not for what He can give us.*" Love, in other words, is a gift.[53] Significantly, Sayers has Jesus make this point while in the midst of recounting to the disciples his temptation in the wilderness (based on Matthew 4 and Mark 4). She thus implies that a fundamental human temptation is to earn power and glory through exchange, as when Satan shows Jesus the great cities of the world, saying "I will give you all these for your own, *if* you will serve me and do homage for them to me."[54] The temptation for Jesus, as for us all, is to mimic the exchangism of other religions.

The Judgment of Sin

If the essence of Christianity is salvation as a gift, not due to exchange lest anyone should boast, what motivation do Christians have to abandon a sinful lifestyle? Why not just accept the gift and keep on making whatever choices we wish? As Paul put it to the Romans, "Should we continue in sin in order that grace may abound?" (6:1).

Sayers took sin seriously—especially her own. Repeatedly she told correspondents that she believed the truth of Christian doctrine because she was convinced about the reality of sin. However, she did not argue that Christians should refrain from sin *in order to* please God and thus avoid God's judgment. Instead, we should refrain from sin due to its dire consequences: not exchangist consequences but natural consequences—consequences, in other words, that God built into the architecture of creation.

Of her preference for the word *consequences* to *punishment*, Sayers writes:

> The word *punishment* for sin has become so corrupted that it ought never to be used. But once we have established the true doctrine of man's nature, the true nature of judgment becomes startlingly clear and rational. . . . In the physical sphere, typhus and cholera are a judgment on dirty living; not because God shows an arbitrary favoritism to nice, clean people, but because of an essential element in the physical structure of the universe.[55]

All too many people, Christians included, think of God as "arbitrary," dreaming up commandments to test people's faith. Instead, as Sayers emphasized repeatedly, God created the universe as good and beautiful, providing an instruction manual (the Bible) about how to maintain the goodness and beauty of creation. Failure to follow the instructions results in adverse, sometimes deadly, consequences. The *consequences themselves* are God's foreordained judgment.

Sayers emphasizes consequences in a series of BBC radio talks about the fundamentals of Christian doctrine, talks that began broadcasting over a year before *The Man Born to Be King* scandalized the nation. In an August 1940 broadcast, Sayers explained, "God never punishes anybody for wrong beliefs—He leaves them to punish themselves"—through the consequences of their actions.[56] And in July of 1941, she asserted,

God's judgments are always the consequences, direct or indirect, of an offence against the universal law: if you hold your hand in the fire, you will be burned; if you swallow prussic acid you will die; if you are wicked and greedy enough to exhaust your soil by over-cropping, the whole country will become a rainless and sandy desert, swept by whirlwinds and barren of food.[57]

Christians, as she goes on to say, unfortunately use the words *divine judgment* in "a very thoughtless and un-Christian sense." In other words, they reduce judgment to an economy of exchange.[58]

Consider this analogy. If you drop your cell phone from the roof of a ten-story building onto the pavement below, chances are it will break. This is not because the manufacturer angrily punishes you in exchange for your carelessness; it is because cell phones weren't made to fall ten floors. Hence, when we throw caution (or our phones) to the wind, disregarding the maker's manual, we experience the consequences of our carelessness.

The parallel applies even to the way humans *respond* to brokenness. Just as some will blame Apple for not making the iPhone strong enough to sustain a ten-story fall, many blame God for their fall from happiness. I once heard a college student whine, "Why does God *do* this to me?!" when her father declined to refill her bank account after she spent her generous allowance on extravagant meals and expensive clothing. This analogy, then, helps explain divine judgment as understood by Sayers. If someone were to sue Apple for the trauma of having a phone break after a ten-story fall, the judge would most likely say that the owner should be held accountable for his own careless behavior rather than blame the maker. The judgment is about the *consequences* of action.

Because we live in a fallen world—fallen far further than ten stories—someone with a clever lawyer might win the lawsuit. But even that fits the analogy. It is well known that rich people who can afford high-powered attorneys often avoid fair judgment for their actions. In light of this fact, we see the brilliance of Christ's famous statement to the rich young man, which Sayers includes in *The Man Born to Be King*: "it is easier for a camel to go through the eye of a needle than for those that set store by riches to enter the kingdom God."[59] Sayers's "set store by" implies that a rich man often thinks according to economies of exchange. Because the wealthy can buy their way out of the consequences of self-serving actions, it is harder for them to see the need for God's *gift* of salvation. This, of course, also explains why we should feel respect for Christians who generously give of their resources to help those who are needy in body, mind, and spirit. Instead of thinking only of themselves, they mirror Christ's gift of salvation.

Predestined Consequences

Even though "nobody can abolish the consequences of sin and error," Sayers explains, "God so works as to redeem the evil by turning it into good."[60] She provides an unusual example of what she means in a letter written to the director of religious broadcasting at the BBC:

> If I get in a rage with you and throw your best teapot out of a window, no amount of forgiveness will unbreak the teapot—all we can aim for is a relationship in which both you and I can bear to sit down and breakfast together out

of a shaving mug without feeling uncomfortable and without an ostentatious avoidance of the subject of teapots. The universe can't "break the iron law of cause and effect"—that would mean an irrational universe; but the effects can be so "made good" that the process is redeemed.[61]

Redemption is not about eliminating consequences; it is about establishing a relationship with the God who created the universe according to certain principles of "cause and effect": a God who wants us to flourish as originally intended, despite the consequences of our actions; a God who will join us at the Communion table to drink Eucharist wine, if even out of a shaving mug.

For Sayers, this is a far preferable way to think of predestination and determinism than the way some Calvinists define them. As she explains, "Some schools of thought assert that . . . everything we do (including Jew baiting in Germany and our own disgusting rudeness to Aunt Eliza) is rigidly determined for us, and that, however much we may dislike the pattern, we can do nothing about it."[62] According to this line of thought, Christians can do nothing even about the people God has foreordained for heaven or for hell. Consider the answer a Sunday school teacher gave to a friend of mine when he was in grammar school. Wracked with worry, the sensitive boy asked, "If God sends everyone to hell that hasn't been born again, what about people in America before missionaries came to tell them about Jesus?" The teacher confidently replied, "Well, it is a matter of predestination. God foreordained who would reject Jesus, putting them in North and South America before missionaries arrived to make sure that they would all go to hell." Hell, for her, was a destination previously established: a pre-destination.

Though most Calvinists are far more sophisticated about the doctrine of predestination than this Sunday school teacher, I still prefer Sayers's sense that foreordained divine judgment is directly tied to Creation: God created a world where actions have predetermined consequences. Nevertheless, God so loved the world that he gave his only begotten son so that we can still have a relationship with our Creator despite those consequences. All we have to do is freely accept the gift of forgiveness that God offers us. This, then, explains the relationship between free will and determinism. As Sayers put it to a scholar interested in Dante's view of hell, "What counts for salvation is the direction of the will. . . . God always puts mercy above justice. You would not accept a last-minute repentance; God will accept anything: His humility is infinite."[63] Mercy is about a gift that lifts us from the muck of sin, whereas justice sinks us deeper into an economy of exchange. Accepting the gift, however, depends upon the direction of one's will.

Direction of the Will

To explore the relationship between free will and God's gift in *The Man Born to Be King*, Sayers once again draws upon an incident recounted only by Matthew, the former tax collector. For her eighth play, she includes Christ's parable about the sheep and the goats (Matthew 25:32–40), having Jesus begin with a statement about the importance of free will: "God will not make any man virtuous by force." And then she has Jesus follow up with his parable: "When the Son of Man comes in glory to judge the world, he will sort them out, as a shepherd sorts out his sheep from the goats." He tells those "on the right hand" that they will "inherit the kingdom," because "when I was hungry and thirsty, you fed me; when I was naked, you clothed me; when I was a stranger, you took me in; when I was sick, you visited me; when I was in prison, you brought me comfort." Sayers naturally knew that such teaching can be reduced to an economy of exchange, whereby people think that certain practices can earn salvation. Hence, as in Matthew's Gospel, she has Jesus establish that those inheriting the kingdom were baffled, asking, "But when, Lord, did we do these things for you?"[64] Oblivious to the fact that they were serving God Incarnate, they clearly were not motivated by what they might get in exchange. Instead, their salvation resulted from the direction of their will: a will that puts the needs of others before their own, as though in silent assent that the universe was created by a loving God who models the gift of mercy.

Sayers continues to follow the biblical account by having the Son of Man next address people whose free will led them in a different direction: "You neither fed nor clothed nor sheltered me, you never helped nor visited me; for when you neglected my brother-men, you neglected me." Jesus closes the parable by suggesting such selfish people "shall go to their long punishment."[65] By choosing self-interest over God's interests, they have *chosen* their own punishment, which is divorce from their Creator. As C. S. Lewis puts it in *The Great Divorce*, a book that Sayers valued, "There are only two kinds of people in the end: those who say to God, 'Thy will be done,' and those to whom God says, in the end, 'Thy will be done.' All that are in Hell, choose it."[66] The same year Lewis published his novel (1946), Sayers said something similar to a correspondent: "The Church cannot, and does not, 'cast' anybody into Hell. People go to Hell because they choose to do so. Hell is the state in which those who choose alienation from God experience the reality of their choice."[67]

Sayers and Lewis thus endorse free will in the midst of God's predetermined created order. The "direction of the will" leads to specific consequences, as when Adam and Eve preferred to grasp after an enticing fruit rather than to be in close relationship with their Creator. But, as the sheep and the goats parable makes clear, "direction of the will" can also lead to positive consequences, because God desires to be in relationship with all of creation.

A Relational God

Christian dogma establishes that God is inherently relational, for God is a Trinity of three persons in one: Father, Son, and Holy Spirit in never-ending relationship. This helps explain why we say "God is love" (1 John 4:8), for love is predicated on relationship rather than an economy of exchange. In her book about the Trinity, *The Mind of the Maker*, Sayers suggests problematic exchangism in anyone who proclaims, "I have sacrificed the best years of my life to my profession (my family, my country, or whatever it may be), and have a right to expect some return." In contrast, "the Christian God is Love" and "the perfect work of love" expects not something in "return" but relationship: "co-operation."[68]

Ironically, the word *relationship* is based on the same Latin root as the word *relativism*: *relatus*. But, as with the words *mercenary* and *mercy*, they have vastly different meanings. God's *mercy* is extended to all those who seek *relationship* with their Creator, whether they have exchanged the right words, rituals, or beliefs: it is about the direction of the will. In this Sayers would agree with C. S. Lewis, whose Narnia stories she valued highly. In March of 1956, Lewis sent her a copy of his newly published *The Last Battle*, which she considered too "terrifying" for young children.[69] But she surely loved the way Lewis dealt with "direction of the will" through Emeth, a follower of the god Tash. Meeting Aslan, the manifestation of God Incarnate in the world of Narnia, Emeth suddenly realizes that he has been worshipping the wrong god his whole life. Aslan assures Emeth, however, that "all the service thou hast done to Tash, I account as service done to me": a clear echo of the sheep and goats parable. However, when Emeth asks if Tash and Aslan "are one," Aslan says, with a growl, "we are opposites." In other words, it is not a matter of exchanging one religion for another, believing that all religions "worship the same God." Such belief reduces worshipping to wor-shopping, making no difference whether one exchanges money for Tide or Wisk. Instead, it's about the earnest desire for God; it's about the direction of the will. As Aslan explains to Emeth, "unless thy desire had been for me thou wouldst not have sought so long and so truly. For all find what they truly seek."[70] It has nothing to do with exchanging the "right" belief for salvation.

Unintended Consequences

Because so many people, believers and skeptics alike, fall into anti-Christ assumptions about the religious importance of exchange, Sayers committed herself to freeing people from pagan notions about earning salvation through rite, ritual, language, or belief. The good news, for her, is *really* good news, news that should be shouted from the rooftops: God, loving the whole world, wants to be in relationship with each and every one of us and therefore offers entirely undeserved salvation from the eternal consequences of sin. However, in order to endorse the inherent goodness of free will, God does not eliminate foreordained, cause-and-effect judgment based on the consequences of choice.

Sayers thought long and hard about God's judgment, due to her own life experience. Following the direction of her will, she suffered profound consequences, confessing in letters discovered decades after her death that, at age thirty, she became pregnant during a rebound relationship with a car salesman who took up with another lover once Sayers's baby came along. Filled with gut-wrenching cynicism, anger, and despair, the confessional letters are addressed to poet and novelist John Cournos, who had refused to have sex with Sayers without birth control, even as Sayers refused to have sex using protection, having been told birth control was a great sin. This stalemate ended their relationship and led to Sayers's rebound affair. Writing to Cournos about the baby and "the beast" who abandoned her, she says, "I've been crying for about three years now": a period of time that includes the dissolution of her relationship with Cournos.[71] Taking a leave of absence from her job at the advertising agency in order to deliver the baby in secret, Sayers placed him in a home for unwanted children run by her cousin. Assuming her parents would be appalled by her ability "to commit so bitter a sin,"[72] Sayers never once told them about the baby. And though they met the boy at their niece's home, the Rev. and Mrs. Sayers died never knowing that they had a grandson.

Sayers's hasty marriage to an older divorced man who had been gassed during World War I intensified the consequences, for one of her primary motivations seems to have been her ability, once married, to adopt the child. After several years, the marriage became difficult due to her husband's PTSD-fueled erratic behavior, and the boy never once entered their home, despite being legally adopted and bearing Sayers's married name: Fleming. Though regularly corresponding with her son, Sayers never informed him that she was his birth mother as well as his adoptive mother.

Nevertheless, Sayers took responsibility for her choices. Making sure the child was well educated, she provided financial support through university and beyond. It wasn't until a dozen years after John's birth, as she was writing *The Zeal of Thy House,* in fact, that she began to free herself from the exchangist notion that she had been "bitterly punished by God" for her sexual decisions.[73]

A Zeal for Consequences: *The Zeal of Thy House*

After agreeing in 1936 to write a play for the Canterbury Festival, Sayers read a Latin history that included William of Sens, the architect hired to reconstruct Canterbury Cathedral after its devastating fire. The author of the history, a monk named Gervase, attributed William's crippling fall from scaffolding "to either the vengeance of God or the envy of the devil."[74] In her play, however, Sayers refuses to endorse Gervase's focus on an economy of exchange, emphasizing, instead, the *consequences* of sin—not only the sin of William's pride, but also the sin of Christian self-righteousness.

Right from the start of *The Zeal of Thy House,* Sayers aligns angels with the consequences of careless actions, having them discuss what caused the fire at Canterbury. A man named Tom Hogg, having neglected the task of cleaning his chimney, caused his thatch roof to catch on fire, sparks from which blew into rafters of the cathedral. When one angel says of the destructive blaze, "A heavy *consequence* for a light offence," another remarks, "I bore the flame betwixt my hands and set it among the rafters."[75] Sayers thus suggests that judgment is manifest through natural consequences, not as God's punishment in exchange for bad behavior.

Meanwhile, Sayers creates a self-righteous monk named Father Theodatus who assesses the fire according to an economy of exchange, arguing that the expense and labor of the new construction is a "reparation" to God, providing "sufficient sacrifice for the sins of this country." Ironically, as Sayers goes on to show, Theodatus fails to think of his own sins, feeling confident that he has done everything necessary to earn God's favor, telling the Prior, "The kingdom of Heaven is *won* by righteousness."[76] The Prior, in contrast, recognizes that salvation from sin is a gift—but a gift that must be accepted in humble acknowledgment that it is entirely undeserved. In response to Theodatus, he states, "I think we sometimes make disasters, and then call them miraculous judgments." A bit later in the same scene he tells others "how sin brings its own suffering,"[77] but, more importantly, that "God's mercy is very great."[78] Perhaps not coincidentally, Sayers has the Prior speak these words of mercy not only to the sexually promiscuous Ursula but also to an innocent "young boy" who has not yet internalized the warped notion that suffering is God's punishment for sin.

In *The Zeal of Thy House*, then, Sayers answers Paul's famous question, "Are we to continue in sin that grace may abound?" with what he says twenty-two verses later: "The wages of sin is death, but the free gift of God is eternal life in Christ Jesus our Lord" (Romans 6:23). Though "wages" implies an economy of exchange, the term "free gift" implies "eternal life" with no strings attached. Sayers deals with the apparent discrepancy by regarding the "wages" of sin as the natural "consequences" of sin. Rather than a payment made by God, as punishment for breaking His law, "death" was the payment made by sin itself, for sin is mired in consequences. Death is merely the natural consequence of sin from which God, through Christ, has saved us—assuming we choose to accept the gift.

By writing *The Zeal of Thy House*, Sayers began to fully internalize the subversive implications of God's gift. Identifying with both William of Sens and Ursula his lover, Sayers recognized that the only unforgivable sin is to reject the gift of forgiveness, offered by a God who wants to be in relationship with every human being, no matter how terrible their mistakes in life. Rejecting the gift is unforgivable because the gift itself is forgiveness. Lack of forgiveness is a judgment based on refusal to accept it. It is a consequence of human choice.

Accepting the Gift

After *The Zeal of Thy House* helped free Sayers from an economy of exchange that had tormented her for much of her life, she exercised her gifts to celebrate God's gift. Leaving behind detective fiction, she dedicated her skills to illuminating how ancient Christian dogma subverts exchangism. By 1941, she actually felt freed enough, and hence free enough, to lecture about how obsession with sexual sins has warped Christian truth: "Perhaps the bitterest commentary on the way in which Christian doctrine has been taught in the last few centuries is the fact that to the majority of people the word *immorality* has come to mean one thing and one thing only." And she gives the example of "a young man who once said to me with perfect simplicity: 'I did not know there were seven deadly sins: please tell me the names of the other six.'"[79]

Before launching into her discussion of the far more deadly sin of Pride, Sayers subversively explains that the Christian obsession with sexual sins has been fed by an economy of exchange: "up till now the Church, in hunting down this sin, has had the active alliance of Caesar, who has been concerned to maintain family solidarity and the orderly devolution of property in the interests of the State."[80] In other words, political leaders endorsed "family values" not for the sake of Christ but to protect private property, knowing that illegitimate children can destabilize the handing over of real estate and political power. Sayers thus illuminates how ancient doctrine becomes compromised when Christians place economic values above Christ. Jesus, of course, not only questioned family values (Luke 14:26), but also repeatedly denounced dependence on property and economies of exchange (Matthew 19:21–26; Luke 12:13–34). Nevertheless, Christians continue to substitute wor-shopping for worshipping, searching Scripture to support economic theories that protect their own best interests, including theories about achieving eternal life through acts of exchange.

Sayers, in contrast, committed herself to weaning Christians from the notion that correct practices or right beliefs are magic coins opening the doors to heaven. Fully believing that "the perfection of God's act doesn't depend on us,"[81] she passionately proclaimed to others God's gift born in a manger. How appropriate, then, that Sayers entered God's presence immediately after shopping for Christmas gifts, having arranged with the stores to mail her purchases directly to friends and family. Imagine the surprise of recipients when, after learning of Sayers's passing, they received her gifts in celebration of Christ's birth. Even after death, Sayers resisted an economy of exchange.

CHAPTER THREE
THE BETRAYAL OF TRADITION, THE TRADITION OF BETRAYAL

Sayers thought a great deal about religious tradition. Convinced that Christian faith must be based on the gift of salvation as outlined in the Nicene Creed, she despaired that Christians who argue the loudest about the importance of tradition often know very little about it. After being attacked for not using King James English in her BBC radio plays about Jesus, she realized that "tradition," for many people, simply means the way their church has said and done things for as long as they can remember.

Sayers found equally disturbing the fact that even defenders of *The Man Born to Be King* seemed oblivious to traditional dogma established at the first four Ecumenical Councils. Often asking Sayers to explain how her *personal* beliefs shaped the radio scripts, such enthusiasts reduced Christianity to religious preference, as though belief were a matter of shopping for the most up-to-date clothes worn by a celebrity author. As Sayers told one longtime friend, "The craze for the 'personal angle' and the 'human touch' is rapidly eating away the brains of the common reader and reducing history to the level of the gossip-column and criticism to something worse. Nobody cares for what is said, but only for the antics of the person who said it."[1]

One need not wonder what she would say about the antics of Christian celebrities that go viral today. Her views are equally applicable to our own era. As she told someone who had endorsed one of her books, "I am weary of this evil and adulterous generation, with its monstrous deification of insignificant personalities. If a thing is not true in itself, the fact that I say it will not make it any truer; nor is it any addition to God that a popular novelist should be so obliging as to approve of Him."[2] Christianity is about accepting God's gift of forgiveness as revealed in the Bible and clarified in the Creeds, not about holding onto traditional practices on the one hand or celebrating the faith of celebrities on the other. Sayers, in fact, deals with both issues in *The Man Born to Be King*, showing how people blind themselves to the gift of salvation and, in the process, end up betraying the truth.

Seeing the Light of Truth

In her seventh play, *The Light and the Life,* Sayers continues to explore the tension between an economy of exchange and God's gift through the story about the man born blind. As she well knew, the account in John's Gospel begins with a classic example of religious exchangism, the disciples asking Jesus, "Rabbi, who sinned, this man or his parents, that he was born blind?" (John 9:2). Sayers slightly expands on this question in her script, using the term "punish" to highlight their warped thinking: "Rabbi Jesus, why was this poor man born blind? Was it to punish some sin of his parents, or did he commit sin himself in a . . . previous existence?"[3] Sayers's added reference to a *previous existence* reinforces her intent, since reincarnation is a classic example of religious exchangism: the things you do in this life will be rewarded or punished by the form you take in the next.

In both the Gospel account and Sayers's play, Jesus replies to the disciples' question about the man born blind by denying an economy of exchange: "Neither he nor his parents are to blame. But it was ordained that the works of God should be shown in him." Jesus then puts mud on the blind man's eyes and directs him to wash in the Pool of Siloam, at which moment the blind man, whom Sayers names Jacob, can see. The "works of God," in other words, are a gift, as Jacob testifies: "Ah! it's a beautiful thing to be able to see the people and the city and the blessed sky and the trees."[4] Jacob's sight makes him aware of the beauty and glory of God's creation.

The local Elders, in contrast, see only the fact that Jesus healed on the Sabbath and thus defied religious law. Angered by anyone who subverts tradition, they accuse Jesus of being "a sorcerer" on the one hand and Jacob of never really being blind on the other.[5] In other words, they come up with multiple reasons to avoid the idea of healing as a gift. For them, following God is all about an economy of exchange: keep the Sabbath and say the proper prayers in order to attain God's blessing in return.

The saddest part of the Gospel account is that Jacob's parents follow the same pattern. Fearing they will be thrown out of the synagogue, they refuse to acknowledge Christ's gift of sight (John 9:21–22). To emphasize this fact, Sayers adds a passage in which Jacob's parents tell their son, "We've been respectable all our lives. I wonder you ain't ashamed to look us in the face"— the irony being that Jacob can, for the first time in his life, *look* them in the face. Using this cliché, Sayers proceeds to question the clichés of tradition. Primarily concerned about conforming to religious practices in order to *look* "respectable," Jacob's parents care more about how they are *seen by* others than about seeing the light—whether the literal light seen by their son or the more subversive spiritual light to which they have been exposed.[6]

After Jacob is thrown out of both the synagogue and his parents' house, Sayers has Jesus approach him while quoting from the first chapter of Genesis: "And God *looked* at everything He had made, and behold! It was very good"—a far cry from Jacob's parents who wondered how the sighted man can now "*look* them in the face." Jesus next asks Jacob, "Are you *glad of the gift* that you found in the Pool of Siloam?" (emphasis mine), and then "If anyone comes to *me, I* will never cast him out" (emphasis Sayers's).[7] Jesus offers the gift of sight to anyone who will accept it, and those who receive it often see how traditional religious practices keep people in the dark. Indeed, when a Pharisee protests because Jacob received sight on the Sabbath, Jesus responds, "You are blind and you insist that you see clearly; that is your sin." This, of course, didn't earn Jesus any favors; but Jesus is not about *earning* favors. Sayers proceeds to end the scene with Christ telling the irate Pharisees, "I know my sheep and am known by them. *My gift to them is eternal life,* and no one can snatch them out of my hand."[8]

After receiving the gift of sight on the Sabbath, the formerly blind Jacob trusts Jesus more than his parents and religious authorities. Betraying tradition, he proceeds to follow his Savior's example by renouncing an economy of exchange. His story, however, should generate a searching question for us today: how do we know which traditions to betray and which to hold onto as the unchanging essence of following Christ? Sayers thought a lot about this question, making it key to the character of Judas in *The Man Born to Be King*.

The Betrayal of Judas

Sayers recognized that Judas could serve as the patron saint of exchangism, having offered up Jesus to political leaders in exchange for thirty pieces of silver. She foreshadows the famous betrayal through a comment made by Matthew not long after Judas first meets Jesus in her fourth radio play. Once complicit with an economy of exchange in his job as tax collector, Matthew describes his former self as "one of the dirty dogs that works for the government and makes his profit out of selling his countrymen"[9]—much as Judas will eventually sell his countryman Jesus. Matthew, of course, turns away from a focus on profit, whereas Judas will go down in history as the most despicable of human beings. Even non-Christians know of his notorious celebrity, aware that the name *Judas* signifies a man who sells out his closest friend: an easy celebrity to despise.

Sayers, however, subverts this traditional view of Judas. Though she follows the biblical account of Judas committing suicide after betraying Jesus with a kiss in the Garden of Gethsemane, in her early plays she establishes that Judas is the most intelligent and committed of all the disciples. The first to recognize that Jesus is the long-awaited Messiah, Judas also realizes that he is a Messiah born to suffer. Judas will do anything to protect Christ's mission, fully believing that humanity can be saved only through sacrifice. As he tells High Priest Caiaphas, Jesus "is the Messiah not of an earthly but of a spiritual Kingdom."[10] Sayers even has Jesus compliment Judas for his impressive "understanding, and courage," calling them "great gifts."[11] Listeners were shocked, some to the point of outrage. Sayers had betrayed tradition about the famous betrayer!

But Sayers was quite intentional in her betrayal. She believed that to make Judas an obvious villain from the start would be an insult to the Son of God. It would imply either that Jesus was not smart enough to recognize Judas's evil intentions, or that he was slyly manipulative, using a despicable man to achieve his own purposes—like something Herod might do. Very early in her writing process she wrote the BBC director of religious programming to explain that Judas "can't have been awful from the start, or Christ would never have called him." And she proceeds to argue that Jesus was too psychologically astute "to have been taken in by an obviously bad hat."[12]

Sayers challenged conventional images of Judas, I believe, for another significant reason. Wanting both skeptics and Christians to see biblical characters as real and hence relatable human beings, she gave Judas a characteristic that tempts and corrupts the most earnest followers of Jesus to this day: certitude.

The Betrayal of Certitude

In contrast to the Jewish Zealots, Sayers's Judas fully understood that Jesus did not come to lead a revolution against Roman oppressors. Convinced the Kingdom of God was to be spiritual, not political, Judas defended Jesus when others questioned his motives. But as Jesus became more and more popular, Judas began to worry that Jesus would abandon the role of suffering servant in order to satisfy his adoring fans. Then something happened that confirmed his suspicions: the triumphal entry of Jesus into Jerusalem (Matthew 21, Mark 11, Luke 19, John 12). Much as politicians today enter rallies with fans cheering and waving signs, Jesus entered the city with admirers yelling "Hosanna" and waving palm branches. As a result, Judas thinks Jesus has fallen for the temptation of celebrity status.

What Judas didn't realize is that a Zealot named Baruch, one of Sayers's most important fictional additions to *The Man Born to Be King,* had contacted Jesus in advance, telling him that if he wanted to fulfill his political role as a revolutionary Messiah, he should ride a horse into Jerusalem. This would signal to the Zealots that Jesus was ready to have warriors follow him into battle in order to overthrow Roman control. But, Baruch adds, if Jesus is too timid to make war against political oppression, he should ride into Jerusalem on a lowly donkey. Judas, of course, saw only the triumphal entry, not realizing the symbolism of Christ choosing the donkey over the horse. Convinced that Jesus has sold out to political celebrity, Judas sells out Jesus to traditionalists.

Sayers's Judas thus acts like many Christians today, certain that *his interpretation* of the truth was absolute—much as those who denounced Jesus for healing on the Sabbath were certain that their understanding of the truth was absolute. The Jesus-following Judas, echoing the anti-Jesus scribes and Pharisees, trusted his own certitude more than he trusted Christ. Sayers thus implies that betraying Jesus for thirty pieces of silver is merely an intensification of the exchange that many Christians fall into. When culture cheers on disturbing new practices, we have a tendency to exchange our trust that Christ is in control for certitude that we know proper biblical behavior, picking and choosing Bible verses that reinforce our certitude. Seeing only the surfaces, we make absolute judgments, believing our certitude is a sign of faith.

The Tradition of Certitude

I speak of certitude from personal experience. In my youth I was certain that Christians who did not baptize through immersion were heretical; Christians who spoke in tongues were demonic; Christians who endorsed the sacraments were superstitious; Christians who drove horse-and-buggies were legalistic; Christians who smoked cigarettes and drank alcohol destroyed the temple of the Holy Spirit; Christians who had icons in their churches were idolatrous. In other words, only the interpretive tradition of my Christian denomination was authentically true.

Clearly, I had totally missed the profundity of Paul's exhortation to the Corinthians: "If I have prophetic powers, and understand all mysteries and all knowledge, and if I have all faith, so as to remove mountains, but have not love, I am nothing." Paul famously ends his sermon about love with, "And now faith, hope, and love abide, these three; and the greatest of these is love" (I Corinthians 13:2, 13). Rather than love, I had made "faith" the "greatest," but only my particular interpretation of "faith"—like Sayers's Judas. Feeling contemptuous of Christians who did not interpret the word of God the way I did, love did not abide with me. Even worse, I had exchanged faith for its exact opposite: certitude. I had made human interpretations more absolute than my Savior, failing to offer the gift of love to those who interpreted Scripture differently. Like Judas, I had betrayed Jesus.

This, of course, was Sayers's point. Christians throughout history have similarly betrayed Jesus. Religious certitude led Christians to denounce and later burn the body of theologian John Wycliffe (1320–1384), not only because he translated parts of the Bible into English, but also because he questioned purgatory, transubstantiation, and other traditional beliefs of his day. Religious certitude led Christians to torture sixteenth-century Anabaptists because the latter believed that baptism should be held off until participants could understand what it meant, a belief that subverted infant baptism, the tradition of their day. Religious certitude caused hundreds of Christians in 1940s England to denounce BBC radio plays about Jesus that failed to use King James English.

Ironically, according to *Strong's Concordance* to the King James Bible, forms of the word *faith* and *faithful* appear around 350 times in Scripture, whereas the word *certitude* appears . . . wait for it . . . not one single time. Even the word *certainty* occurs a mere seven times, and, of its three instances in the New Testament, only one reference has to do with certainty about the Gospel message (Luke 1:4). The discrepancy, of course, is easy to explain: God calls us to faith, which is the opposite of certitude. And greater than both is love—at least according to the apostle Paul and confirmed by the sacrificial love delineated in the Nicene Creed.

Through the character of Judas, then, Sayers illustrates her own suspicions about certitude, perhaps because certitude reinforces an economy of exchange. Sayers has the disciple Matthew decline to handle the disciples' money as part of his repudiation of a life dedicated to exchangism. Taking over the role of disciple treasurer is, of course, Judas. Sayers keeps reminding us of his economic status, as in the play containing Christ's feeding of the five thousand, appropriately titled *The Bread of Heaven*. After Judas protests that they don't have enough money to buy food for that many people, Jesus states, "Well, we must do the best and trust to God." Jesus, in other words, advocates trust and love over economic certainty. What follows is a gift even more extravagant than the one at Cana. Rather than turning water into wine, this time Jesus turns five loaves and two fish into a meal for thousands, after praying, "Father of all goodness, we thank Thee for Thy *gifts*."[13] Both miracles anticipate the greatest gift of all, when Christ explains at the Last Supper that His blood and body, represented by wine (like that at Cana) and bread (like that which fed the five thousand), will be offered as a gift for our salvation.

Though Judas witnessed these amazing miracles, he handed over Jesus to traditionalists who preferred an economy of exchange to God's gift.

Handing Over Tradition

Fourteen years after *The Man Born to Be King* outraged traditionalists all over England, Sayers delivered a lecture that included this interesting fact: the word *tradition* comes from a Latin root that means "handing over."[14] Indeed, traditions are the established beliefs and practices that are handed over from one generation to the next in order to preserve them. Ironically, however, words that share the same root as *tradition* all have to do with the concept of betrayal. *Treason*, *traitor*, and *traduce* all signal the handing over of someone or something to an enemy—as Judas handed over Jesus to disgruntled traditionalists. What could *tradition* and *treason* possibly have in common?

As Sayers well knew, "handing over" a tradition often changes it as the next generation makes it relevant to their lives, thus betraying, or handing over, original expressions or meanings. This is certainly what Jesus did to the traditional significance of the Sabbath, as well as to the traditional meaning of the Messiah, which led many devout followers of God to believe he was a *traitor* to their faith.

The positive and negative meanings of *handing over* appear in Greek as well. Authors of the New Testament employ the same Greek root to describe not only Judas's "handing over" of Christ to religious authorities, but also the "handing over" of Christ's words to his followers. The apostle Paul puns on the words in his first letter to the Corinthians: "For I received from the Lord what I also *handed over* to you, that the Lord Jesus on the night when he was *handed over* took bread and when he had given thanks, he broke it, and said, 'This is my body which is for you. Do this in remembrance of me'" (11:23–24, my transliteration). Think of Paul's wordplay here: Christ was handing over to his disciples the truth about his being handed over to petty politicians, and his handed-over body would soon be handed over to Christians through reenactments of the Last Supper. Paul, in fact, was handing over that truth to the Corinthians—and to us as we read our Bibles—which inevitably results in *betrayal*. Indeed, most Roman Catholics believe that Protestants have *betrayed* Eucharist by handing it over to meanings that do not include the doctrine of transubstantiation.[15]

The same might be said of handing over the Bible. Before the invention of the printing press, handwritten Bibles were so expensive that many small churches could not afford to own a single one. Interpretation was therefore, by cultural necessity, established by Christian leaders—like the Pope and his cardinals in the Western church—who, after determining the best Christian practices, communicated them to priests, who handed them over to their parishioners. However, once the printing press made Bibles affordable, such that all literate Christians could read

Scripture on their own, Martin Luther could betray the authority of the Pope and his bishops by handing over Bible interpretation to "the priesthood" of *all* believers. Wanting to make the Bible available for an even greater number of Christians, Luther did something even more subversive: he translated it into German. A tradition of biblical authority was "handed over" to a new generation, which, due to changes in culture, betrayed the priesthood of the Catholic hierarchy. Luther was therefore excommunicated from the Roman Church much as Sayers's Jacob, the man born blind, was "excommunicated" from the Synagogue for betraying religious authority.[16] In both instances, traditionalists regarded the new practices as treasonous.

Ironically, as Luther and Sayers both knew, it is treason that keeps tradition alive.

Consider, for example, the selling of indulgences that Luther protested. The idea of God's indulgence is as essential to Christian doctrine as is the central arch of a cathedral: God indulges believers with the undeserved, unmerited gift of salvation. Over the centuries, however, God's indulgence fell into an economy of exchange, as often happens with traditional teaching. Christians started believing that certain practices were *required* in order to *earn* God's indulgence: say this many Hail Marys; donate this much money to the cathedral; make a pilgrimage to Jerusalem; kiss this reliquary that contains the bone of a saint. Then, due to the development of the printing press, wily entrepreneurs were able to mass-produce certificates, enabling Christians with money to literally buy "indulgence" papers that would guarantee them swifter passage through purgatory. A doctrinal arch of Christianity had fallen into ruin, compelling Luther to replace it before the whole church fell down.

The Purging of Purgatory

Sayers was intrigued by the tradition of purgatory—as was C. S. Lewis, who loved her translation of Dante's *Purgatorio*, published by Penguin Books. Developed by the church relatively early in its history, purgatory was suggested by a statement Paul makes to the Corinthians while discussing bodily resurrection: "Otherwise, what will those people do who receive baptism on behalf of the dead? If the dead are not raised at all, why are people baptized on their behalf?" (I Corinthians 15:29).[17] In response to this verse, Christians developed a conceptual schema explaining baptism for the dead. That schema, of course, was purgatory: a place between heaven and hell where the dead, aided by the prayers of the living, can purge their sins as they take an arduous path leading to paradise.

Sayers spent the last thirteen years of her life studying, translating, lecturing on, and writing about Dante's *Divine Comedy*, which consists of *Inferno*, *Purgatorio*, and *Paradiso*. In the introduction to her translations, however, she explicitly states, "We must try to believe that man's will is free, that he can consciously exercise choice, and that his choice can be decisive to all eternity."[18] Repeatedly emphasizing that *The Divine Comedy* dramatizes human choice rather than God's punishment, Sayers seeks to purge purgatory, as well as heaven and hell, of traditional associations with exchangism. In one of her many lengthy letters to Charles Williams, whose book *The Figure of Beatrice* (1943) ignited her interest in *The Divine Comedy*, she explains how satisfying she found Dante's emphasis on human will: "instead of being formally allotted so much pains and penalties and ceremonially let off the chain at the end of it," spirits making their way through purgatory "simply know when they've finished by feeling themselves all right. It gets rid of all that awful deadening stuff about arbitrary punishment."[19] As far as Sayers was concerned, to criticize someone for believing in purgatory is like criticizing someone for choosing to bathe before meeting royalty: based on traditional practices, the bather sees it as a necessary step in preparation to meet the king.

The problem, of course, is that both supporters and detractors have reduced purgatory to a simplistic economy of exchange. Sayers therefore explicitly states in the introduction to her *Purgatorio* translation, "Purgatory is not a system of Divine book-keeping—so many years for so much sin—but a process of spiritual improvement which is completed precisely when it is complete." And she proceeds to quote Charles Williams: "God is satisfied when we are satisfied."[20] Furthermore, Sayers implies that this was Dante's view as well, following up a quotation from his *Purgatorio* with this statement: "There is no point, you see, at which God says: 'Your term's up,' or . . . 'I have received a great many prayers and offerings on your behalf, so I'll let you off the rest.'"[21] It's not about exchange, lest anyone should boast. Some readers, of course, may assume that Dante, Williams, and Sayers dishonor the ancient tradition of purgatory, but Sayers proves that Dante's idea is nothing new. She does so by quoting second-century theologian Origen, who says of purgatory, "These souls receive in prison, not the retribution of their folly; but a benefaction in the purification from the evils contracted in that folly; a purification effected by the means of salutary troubles."[22]

Unfortunately, despite their biblically based profundity, traditions like purgatory often fall into exchangism. Such traditions must therefore be handed over to new meanings that reignite ancient truths, purging them of anti-Christian assumptions. Sayers understood this long before she started translating Dante. In 1941, while addressing the Archbishop of York's conference at Malvern, she defined "a Church" as a body of humans "organized within a *living tradition* whose essence persists unchanged while its expressions continually develop, by a single devotion and a single service to an immanent and transcendent reality, whose claims are felt to be paramount."[23] The essence persists—is handed over through the centuries—even as its expressions are handed over to new meanings, not in spite of but due to our devotion and service to the unchanging reality of a both/and God: both immanent and transcendent. Roman Catholic cardinal Henri de Lubac would agree, suggesting in 2006 that "Preserving the status quo in theories and viewpoints has never been and can never be an adequate means of safeguarding the truth."[24] Truth must be handed over. This, of course, sometimes results in the abandonment of thousand-year-old traditions altogether, as with Protestant responses to the doctrine of purgatory.

Betraying Traditional Music

For a more recent example of handing over, let's consider something Sayers valued highly: music. As a youth she played the violin, and one of the highlights of her college years was singing in the Oxford University Bach Choir. I am sure she would be intrigued by what happened to church music not long after she fell to her death at the bottom of a staircase. In 1957, the year she died, a group of British musicians formed a rock band that eventually took on the name the Beatles. Hundreds of churchgoers later felt betrayed as younger generations handed over worship music to instruments and rhythms they associated with the Beatles and other rock groups.

Ironically, Christians who wanted to purge the church of drums and electric guitars did not realize that the organ music they regarded as sacred tradition was once considered too secular for churches. Tradition, for them, meant only what they had always done. Baptist Minister of Music Charles Keown provides a good example, quoting from a letter written by a worshipper who felt betrayed by contemporary music: "What is wrong with the inspiring hymns with which we grew up? When I go to church, it is to worship God, not to be distracted with learning a new hymn. Last Sunday's was particularly unnerving. The tune was un-singable and the new harmonies were quite distorting." Keown proceeds to explain that the letter from the annoyed worshipper was written in 1890 about the hymn "What a Friend We Have in Jesus."[25]

As with Tyndale's translations used in the King James Bible and Sayers's betrayal of Tyndale in *The Man Born to Be King*, something denounced in one era is sanctified in the next. For this very reason Sayers emphasized the need for Christians to study history in order to recognize the various ways tradition has always been betrayed. In her terms, churches today keep the *essence* of worship alive by celebrating sounds of electric guitars as new *expressions* of traditional praise to Jesus Christ.

Living the Essence

Despite this assurance, we are still left with an important question: how do we know which traditions to purge and which to hold onto as the unchanging *essence* of Christianity? On one level Sayers's answer is simple. Anytime we reduce Christian belief and practices to an economy of exchange we destabilize the distinctive essence of Christianity: the non-negotiable truth that salvation through the death and resurrection of Christ is a gift. Any handing over that undermines dogma about God's gift, as delineated in the first four Ecumenical Councils, should be avoided.

The issue, of course, is far more complex than simply confirming the Nicene Creed. Fortunately, Sayers had more to say. Here, then, is how I would summarize her understanding of Christianity's "*living tradition,* whose essence persists unchanged while its expressions continually develop":

1. The truth of salvation through Christ, proclaimed in the New Testament and explained at the first four Ecumenical Councils, *does not change,* but the way Christians *interpret and apply the truth* changes as human contexts change.

2. To make one interpretation of the truth absolute is to act like Judas, who, oblivious to cultural contexts, believed that only he recognized correct behavior.

3. Rather than be intimidated or outraged by differing interpretations of the truth, we should celebrate how difference affirms the incarnation: God's endorsement of the flesh.

4. As with the man born blind, the emphasis should always be on seeing Jesus and following his example rather than on looking for ways to maintain what we blindly consider irrefutable truth.

Changing interpretations of the atonement illustrate how Sayers understood and practiced the handing over of tradition.

Handing Over the Atonement

Not long after *The Zeal of Thy House* reignited her interest in theology, Sayers published an article that parodied how people understood basic Christian doctrines, including the atonement. Using a question and answer format, she writes:

Q.: What is meant by the Atonement?

A.: God wanted to damn everybody, but His vindictive sadism was sated by the crucifixion of His own Son, who was quite innocent, and, therefore, a particularly attractive victim. He now only damns people who don't follow Christ or who never heard of Him.[26]

Originally defined as "the removal of human sin as a hindrance to relationship with God,"[27] the atonement has been reduced, in many people's minds, to an economy of exchange.

In response, Sayers handed over the atonement to new expressions in *The Man Born to Be King*. As actors were in rehearsal for the twelfth and final radio broadcast, one approached Sayers to tell her "That's the first time I've ever heard the Atonement explained—so as to mean anything, that is."[28] Even though atonement through Christ's resurrection is the *essence* of Christianity, the actor did not consider it comprehensible until Sayers gave it new *expression*.

The illuminating scene for the actor was one in which Sayers has the resurrected Jesus show his pierced hands and feet to Doubting Thomas. Borrowing a verse from the Gospel of John (20:29), Sayers has Jesus state, "Blessed are they that have not seen, and yet have believed." But then Sayers adds dialogue from other disciples. James recounts all the ways Jesus suffered brutalizing torture in order to ask, "Is that what we do to God?" John follows up by inverting the final question, asking Jesus, "Beloved, when you patiently suffered all things, and went down to death with all our sins heaped upon you—is that what God does for us?"[29] Sayers's point is that the crucifixion of Jesus was not done *in exchange for* human sin. Instead, our sins, like those of Judas, murdered God Incarnate—"what we do to God"—who defeated death through the resurrection: "what God does for us."

Sayers thus shows Christ's disciples learning how to maintain belief in the atonement while purging it of exchangism. Significantly, the definition quoted above, "removal of human sin as a hindrance to relationship with God," refers to the Old Testament view of atonement: a tradition Christians maintain while handing it over to new meanings. As Jesus himself put it during the Sermon on the Mount, "Do not think that I have come to abolish the law or the prophets; I have come not to abolish but to fulfill" (Matthew 5:17). The essence of Yom Kippur—the Day of Atonement—persists even as a new expression fulfills it. Indeed, Church dogma establishes that Jesus Christ is the *essence* of God *expressed* in new form: human flesh.

Once again, Sayers returns Christians to the need for education, encouraging us to study the history of dogma to discover how the essence of atonement truth persists, even as its expressions develop. What follows is a brief introduction to changing views of the atonement, changes that exposed, for Sayers, the double meaning of "handing over."

Christian Atonement Theories

Two hundred years after the resurrected Jesus appeared to Doubting Thomas, church leaders were describing Christ's death as a "ransom" that God paid to Satan, who had kidnapped humanity. Seeking to save humanity from Satan's clutches, God paid the ransom by sending Jesus to the cross. As the ransom theory evolved, it developed an even more disturbing bait-and-switch element. God baited Satan by offering Christ's death as ransom, snatching the ransom back by resurrecting Jesus from the dead. It was like a scene from a movie in which money paid to a kidnapper goes up in smoke as soon as the briefcase holding it is opened. The kidnapper of humanity is left with an empty briefcase just as Roman and Jewish authorities were left with an empty tomb.

Sayers despaired over the propensity to turn Satan into a person who nearly gets the better of God. For her, it reeks of Manichaeism, a heresy that she mentions repeatedly in her writings. The third-century Iranian prophet who influenced the heresy, Mani, held that "the task of religion was to release the particles of light which Satan stole from the realm of light and imprisoned in the human brain."[30] For Mani, then, the body is evil, while the spiritual realm of light is a good that must be released from the body's prison. Sayers, however, asserted that Christians should "have nothing to do with those religions which teach that the body is evil, or that matter is evil," and she goes on to connect this belief with problematic views of Satan's near equality with God: "God is a Person; but it is scarcely accurate to say that there is a 'personal' Devil, for evil breaks up the personality. Of that proud spirit there is now nothing left but a ravenous, chaotic will, a motiveless and unmeaning malice, at once cunning and witless." Rather than a spiritual person, spiritual pride prevents people from humbly submitting their wills to God.[31]

Sayers, of course, was not the first to question Satan's involvement in the atonement. The English town of Canterbury, where her life was transformed, became identified with the handing over of atonement theory to a new expression. Known as the "satisfaction theory," the new expression was developed by Anselm of

Canterbury (1033–1109), who argued that God was dishonored when humanity chose sin over obedience. Someone must therefore pay a price to satisfy God's honor, but the price is so high that no human can possibly pay it. Only God in human form can make a payment great enough to restore God's honor. Alister McGrath suggests that this "satisfaction" theory of atonement might derive "from the Germanic laws of the period, which stipulated that an offense had to be purged through an appropriate payment."[32]

Clearly, this theory still perpetuates what Sayers considered "disgusting ideas about 'satisfaction' and 'paying off.'"[33] Whereas the ransom theory had God enter an economic transaction with Satan, Anselm's theory has Jesus function like a medieval knight who is required to give up his life in order to make satisfactory payment to his feudal lord. As Roman Catholic theologian Richard Viladesau notes, Anselm's theory ended up reinforcing a "commercial" approach to salvation, where Christians would "*pay* to have a certain number of masses celebrated," or even "*pay someone else* to satisfy one's penitential obligation," thus using money to buy their way into heaven.[34] The buying and selling of indulgences was merely an extension of an exchangist interpretation of atonement, once again reducing Christianity to the level of all other religions. Indeed, as Sayers notes in her introduction to *The Man Born to Be King*, the words *substitution* and *propitiation* were appropriated from "older religions."[35]

Committed to maintaining the unique essence of Christianity—salvation as a gift—Sayers preferred theories of atonement emphasizing that Jesus voluntarily paid the price for salvation. If someone pays off your mortgage, with no strings attached, it is a gift to you. (Isn't it interesting that, in the realm of finance, people still use language about "forgiving a debt"?)

Out of sheer love, Jesus gave his life to redeem us (forgive us) from the mortgage (the debt) of our sins: it is a totally undeserved gift.

Nevertheless, language about "paying off" can still perpetuate a problematic view of God that turns people away from accepting the gift of forgiveness. Writing to a Catholic theologian who had praised her work, Sayers despairs that skeptics assume Christians believe

> that Jehovah (the old man with the beard) made the world and made it so badly that it all went wrong and he wanted to burn it up in a rage; whereat the Son (who was younger and nicer, and not implicated in his Father's irresponsible experiment) said: "Oh, don't do that! if you must torment somebody, take it out [on] me." So Jehovah vented his sadistic appetite on a victim who had nothing to do with it all, and thereafter grudgingly allowed people to go to heaven if they provided themselves with a ticket of admission signed by the Son.[36]

Lest you think that Sayers is being offensive in her exaggeration, she continues with, "This grotesque mythology is not in the least exaggerated: *it is what they think we mean*" (emphasis hers). I can verify the relevance of her statement to our own era. In the last several years, one college professor told me that Christian teaching about God's sacrifice of his Son "promoted child abuse." And I have heard some theologians argue that we need to get rid of talk about the atonement due to its "sadism." In contrast, Sayers would argue that what we need to get rid of, instead, is language about "satisfaction and paying off" that has turned Christianity into one among many exchangist religions. What we need is to hand over the atonement to the shock of the old: salvation as a payment-free gift.

Fleshing Out the Atonement

My brief summation of two very different atonement theories provides enough background to return us to the central issue of this chapter: changes in Christian tradition. How might Sayers help us know which Christian traditions—at least those developed after the first four Ecumenical Councils laid the unmovable foundation of orthodox faith—best capture the essence of Christianity?

To a certain extent, Sayers has already provided an answer about what *not* to do. Her BBC radio renditions of Jacob, the man born blind, and Judas, the betrayer of Christ, provide cautionary tales. Whereas her latter characterization warns us against arrogant certitude that we know which interpretations of truth are always correct, Sayers uses the parents of Jacob to exemplify self-serving endorsements of tradition that blind people to the subversive work of God Incarnate. Jacob, in contrast, looks to Jesus, the author and finisher of his sight.

By looking to Jesus, Sayers can celebrate "a living tradition whose essence persists unchanged while its expressions continually develop": a living tradition that she illustrates with atonement theory. As she recounts to a famous Dante scholar:

> Atonement metaphors vary from century to century according to social changes. In St. Paul's time, the metaphor is predominantly that of deliverance from bondage—naturally enough, in a period when slavery was a universal fact. In the mediaeval West, with its strongly juridical mind, we get the

idea of the Devil's contract, from which the soul has to be released—or—since nearly everybody seemed to be in the hands of money lenders—the metaphor of the unpayable debt. . . . They are all scriptural, but each has its special appeal to a different age. They agree that something is done for Man which he could not do for himself.[37]

By arguing this way, Sayers endorses the teaching of the Ecumenical Councils, which emphasize the incarnation: God taking on flesh to enter into history. Flesh is always influenced by the time and place where it is located. It would be just as absurd to assert that Christians throughout history thought exactly the same about the atonement as it would be to suggest that Jesus used a GPS device to get him from Jerusalem to Nazareth. Instead, God in the flesh dressed, ate, and traveled the way most people in his culture did.

Despite the differing ways various cultures have understood the atonement, all recognize the same truth: salvation is something done for humans that they cannot do for themselves. God's truth does not change, but human understanding changes as culture changes; to deny this is to proclaim a Judas-like certitude that one's own culture has fully attained the mind of God, which is the ultimate blasphemy. Even Jesus, once he became flesh, did not entirely know the mind of God, evident in several comments he made, such as his reference to the passing away of heaven and earth: "But about that day and hour no one knows, neither the angels of heaven, nor the Son, but only the Father" (Matthew 24:36). Christ's prayer in the Garden of Gethsemane (Matthew 26, Mark 14, Luke 22) implies, as well, that Jesus did not fully understand the implications of God's plan.

In her *Man Born to Be King* rendition of the Gethsemane prayer, Sayers has Jesus say, "Abba, Father—all things are possible with Thee. If it be possible, let this cup pass from me. . . . If it be possible—nevertheless, not as I will, but as Thou wilt." Though very close to the synoptic Gospel accounts, Sayers has Jesus repeat the word *possible* three times, as though to emphasize that Christ, like any fully human individual, does not want to suffer torture and death. After Jesus discovers the disciples asleep, she follows with a statement that appears only in Matthew: "The Spirit, indeed, is willing, but the flesh is weak" (Matthew 26:41). But then she has Jesus say immediately afterward, "Do I not know it?" as though to once again emphasize that he is as human as they.[38]

Mirroring the Truth

All humans see truth through a mirror that reflects their humanity: fleshly bodies embedded in a certain era and location. As Paul put it, "For now we see in a mirror, dimly, but then we will see face to face. Now I know only in part; then I will fully, even as I have been fully known" (I Corinthians 13:12). God's truth doesn't change, but our understanding of it changes as the mirror of culture changes, necessitating its handing over to new meanings in order to illuminate its truth for new generations. As far as Sayers was concerned, this is true even about some of the ancient creeds.

Take, for example, how Sayers dealt with a line from the Apostles' Creed: "He *descended* into Hell." Left out of the Nicene Creed, the sentence reflects the fleshly understanding of early Christians, who assumed hell was underneath the ground where they buried their dead: a *descent* into deeper parts of the earth.

Today, our geological knowledge of the earth's core makes this idea seem like something out of fantasy fiction: descending to a burning place in the middle of the earth, an idea that became embellished with images of pointy-tailed demons poking the damned with pitchforks: a tradition that Dante handed over by turning the center of hell into ice. Nevertheless, rather than abandon the doctrine of hell, we might follow the example of Sayers, who confirms the "*living tradition* whose essence persists unchanged while its expressions continually develop."

In an article commissioned a year before she died, Sayers grappled with belief about heaven and hell, starting with the words, "If we are to understand the Christian doctrine about what happens at death, we must first rid our minds of every concept of time and space as we know them."[39] In other words, it is naïve to locate hell in the *space* of our earth, or to think of heaven as bliss extended in *time*, because God, who created space and time at the moment of creation, transcends both.

Eternity, Sayers makes clear, is not about time. Heaven is about being in the presence of God, whereas hell is utter separation from God. Both are outside the space/time continuum, and both are the result of choosing to accept a gift, like that accepted by the man born blind. As Sayers emphatically puts it:

> God sends nobody to Hell; only a wicked ignorance can suggest that He would do to us the very thing He died to save us from. But He has so made us that what in the end we choose, that in the end we shall have. If we enter the state called Hell, it is because we have willed to do so.[40]

The idea of God sending people to hell reflects an economy of exchange similar to that of other religions: when individuals displease the gods they get unending torture in exchange. The concept of hell is therefore attractive to pious people who resent (and perhaps secretly envy) indulgent sinners: an attitude that Sayers calls "a sadistic 'compensation-fantasy.'"[41] Such people want to believe their piety has earned them a better reward than a God-defying skeptic, their restraint and discipline functioning like a "Get Out of Jail Free" card from Monopoly: a game based on finance and exchange. What the pious should desire, instead, is to be in relationship with Creator God outside of space and time—a blessing available to anyone who chooses to accept the unmerited offer of God's love.

When it comes to changes in culturally constructed theories about hell and the atonement, then, Sayers would have Christians endorse views that avoid what she calls the "unpleasantly 'mercantile' implications of the 'debt' metaphor."[42] More importantly, she would emphasize that God's gift was made available to the whole world when Jesus rose from the dead—whether he "descended" or not. The crucial doctrine of Christ's death and resurrection, affirmed by the earliest Creeds, does not change, even when interpretations of how it functions—as in how the atonement works—change over time. Truth, like Jesus Christ, is both/and: both tradition and change.

Quantum Leaps of Change: Science versus Faith

Many people religiously idealize change, advocating progress as a good in and of itself. Sayers, however, believed that those who think progress entails renouncing ancient creeds are not that much different from the Christians who denounced her colloquial radio plays. Like Judas, both make *their* interpretations of reality absolute: many 1940s Christians had certitude that only the "Authorized Version" of the Bible infallibly captured truth, while many 1940s skeptics, regarding the "authority" of scientists "almost infallible," as Sayers puts it, had certitude that science, and science only, captures truth about life.[43]

In contrast, Sayers champions not only change made through scientific discoveries but also the unchanging truth of the Nicene Creed, endorsing her both/and thought by establishing similarities between science and religion. As she well knew, scientific hypotheses are proposed and maintained by faith, sometimes generating as much controversy among professional scientists as issues of Christian belief have generated among professional theologians.

Sayers would be delighted that quantum physics provides an apt example. In 1944, while responding to a correspondent who evidently thought that evidence of multiple universes undermined Christianity, she brought up current scientific data about quantum leaps: the sudden change in the energy level of electrons as they "orbit" atoms. Putting it in the popular terms of her day, she states, "the whole universe of material phenomena is controlled, according to the physicist, by the orbit-jump of the atom: a thing so small that no eye can perceive it, and so obscure and intangible that nobody can say rightly whether it is properly to be called a 'thing' at all."[44] Because no unaided eye can perceive sub-atomic particles, Sayers suggests, we must take on faith the authority of scientists who have recorded evidence of quantum leaps, much as we take on faith the authority of bishops at the Ecumenical Councils. And we must remember that sometimes scientific interpretations of "obscure and intangible" phenomena are revised— much as Christian theories of the atonement have been revised.

Indeed, less than a decade after Sayers wrote about "orbit-jumps," Albert Einstein and Erwin Schrödinger stunned scientists by arguing against the theory of instantaneous "quantum leaps" as proposed by scientific greats Niels Bohr and Werner Heisenberg. They did so around the same time Sayers was stunning Christians with *The Emperor Constantine* (1951), her historical play about the debate between Athanasius, who argued that Jesus was fully God, and Arius who used Scripture to argue that Jesus was God's creation. Like brilliant scientists, brilliant theologians often disagree about theories of truth.

Sayers, of course, knew that science and religion are not the same. Whereas we have no way to prove that the Son was one substance with the Father as argued by Athanasius, experimentation can prove scientific theories true or false. Nevertheless, truths that scientists emphatically endorse in one era can be overturned by the next. For example, scientific teams in 1986 and 2007 declared they found empirical proof for instantaneous quantum leaps by subatomic particles: evidence that undermined the arguments of Einstein and Schrödinger. In 2019, however, researchers at Yale challenged the long-held belief in quantum leaps by witnessing, with more sophisticated technological devices, the slow development of subatomic change, thus subverting the theory of spontaneous quantum "leaps."[45] This only goes to show that people who say "I will believe in nothing but what I can see and handle" are naïve about how much seeing and handling rely on faith, not only faith in the latest technology, but also faith in scientific predecessors.

Ironically, the statement "I will believe in nothing but what I can see and handle" is spoken by Judas in *The Man Born to Be King*.[46] Certain that he knew the proper behavior of the Messiah,

Judas anticipates those scientists who, by validating quantum leaps, felt certain about the proper behavior of subatomic particles.

The Man Born to Be Reasonable

This is not at all to say that Sayers sneered at science as did some Christians of her generation. She, in fact, satirized the way believers often define faith as "resolutely shutting your eyes to scientific fact," and intellect as "a barrier to faith."[47] Valuing evidence gleaned from laboratory experimentation, she hired a professional scientist to help her with details for one of her detective novels, *The Documents in the Case* (1930). And she was so careful with the chemistry in *Strong Poison* (1930) that an Oxford-educated scientist wrote her to say he was quoting from the novel approvingly in his book *Chemistry: The Conquest of Materials* (1957).[48] But Sayers also respected Christianity enough to argue that it was as rationally cogent as science. Soon after *The Zeal of Thy House* reignited her intellectual engagement with orthodoxy, Sayers argued that "every theoretical scheme demands the acceptance of some postulate or other."[49]

Skeptics with the certitude of Judas, of course, disdain such an idea. One listener who tuned in to *The Man Born to Be King*, for example, was appalled that Sayers's scripts seemed to endorse the miracles of Jesus. Expecting the scandalous plays to expose supernaturalism as naïve, he wrote an irate letter to Sayers:

> I heard part of your radio play last night, but eventually switched off in disgust that such drivel should be given over the air. . . . I can quite understand people of little education accepting and taking in such things as these, but you must have

made research and enquiries into the actual so-called miracle [at Cana] and in view of your findings, I cannot understand why you should then write a play based on a pack of lies.[50]

Sayers wrote him back, a bit testy about his sneering attitude: "I am sorry that you should have sustained such a shock. Is this really the first time you have realised that quite a large number of educated persons profess the Catholic Faith?" (by which she meant Christian orthodoxy based on the Creeds).[51] Her letter shocked him again, as he readily admits: "I actually did not think you would trouble to reply. I usually find that religious followers are quite content to sit smugly behind their Bible, and refuse to answer questions"[52]—something that continues to happen today.

Sayers, in contrast, kept writing to the skeptic, named L. T. Duff, to explain what Christian orthodoxy really teaches, as well as to show what it has in common with science:

> One act of faith must, indeed, be made before one can accept Christianity: one must be prepared to believe that the universe is rational, and that (consequently) human reason is valid so far as it goes. But that is an act of faith which we have to make in order to think about anything at all. . . . Admittedly, we cannot prove that the universe is rational; for the only instrument by which we can prove anything is reason, and we have to assume the rationality of things before we can trust or use our reason. But every act and word of our daily life—not to mention all art and science—are based on that assumption; without that act of faith we could not live or act.[53]

Sayers's correlation between faith, art, and science has been confirmed by many scientists. Fifty years after Sayers made her statement to L. T. Duff, Robert Wright, a self-identified secular humanist who has taught science and religion at Ivy League universities, published these words:

> The theory of natural selection is so elegant and powerful as to inspire a kind of faith in it—not *blind* faith, really, since the faith rests on the theory's demonstrated ability to explain so much about life. But faith nonetheless; there is a point after which one no longer entertains the possibility of encountering some fact that would call the whole theory into question. . . . I admit to having reached this point.[54]

Sayers would claim the same for Christianity, saying her faith rests in its demonstrated ability to explain so much about life.

Because faith is fundamental to all knowledge, people suspicious of Christian miracles, like L. T. Duff, have much to learn about the way faith affects science, just as Christians have much to learn about the way science affects belief. It is no coincidence that theology was once called "the Queen of the Sciences," for the word *science* simply means *knowledge*: knowledge that might change, like knowledge about the relation of the earth to the sun or knowledge about sudden quantum leaps. Nevertheless, as Sayers argues to the anti-miracle Duff, many people maintain a superstitious belief in "Science" with a capital *S*, trusting "that any 'scientist' can produce a 'scientific' opinion on any subject, whether it is *his* subject and *his* science or not."[55] Sayers thus suggests that people like Duff merely turn science into an alternative religion.

Anti-miracle skeptics and anti-science Christians, then, are opposite sides of the same coin: promoters of either/or thought. In contrast, Sayers suggests that Christians who endorse both/and knowledge described by the ancient creeds intelligently consider new scientific theories while simultaneously endorsing a reality that transcends empirical experimentation. Christians who believe in miracles, in fact, are often *more* open-minded than people who deny the possibility of supernatural events, because they think in both/and terms. Indeed, skeptics can be so prejudiced against the very concept of the supernatural that they refuse to take seriously any evidence of miracles. Granted, as Sayers would be the first to admit, many proclaimed miracles are bogus. But she also knew that to universalize from bad examples is a form of bigotry, reflecting one's bias more than reality. As she puts it to the miracle-scoffing Duff, "if anybody begins a sentence 'Science says . . .' or 'Science has proved . . .' he betrays an anthropomorphic tendency which needs to be checked by the question: 'Which science?' and indeed, 'Which scientists?'"[56]

Changing Knowledge

Nevertheless, scientists are often more open to reconsidering their knowledge than are religious people, as Sayers discovered most dramatically when Singapore's fall to Japanese forces in 1942 was proclaimed to be God's retribution for her subversive radio plays about Jesus. Christians keep returning to an economy of exchange because it's so much easier to understand: *If* you do this/ believe this/practice this *Then* you get salvation (or retribution) in exchange; case closed. Confident they have followed the right formula, exchangists take comfort in what Sayers calls "pious phrases and reverent language,"[57] not having to think about what a radical idea the murder of God truly is. As she comments to the BBC director of religious programming in the middle of the *Man Born to Be King* scandal:

123

Nobody cares a dump nowadays that Christ was "scourged, railed upon, buffeted, mocked, and crucified," because all those words have grown hypnotic with ecclesiastical use. But it does give people a slight shock to be shown that God was flogged, spat upon, called dirty names, slugged in the jaw, insulted with vulgar jokes, and spiked up on the gallows like an owl on a barn-door.[58]

Notice how Sayers's word choice makes the story more shocking—which is precisely her point. As she emphatically puts it, "Shocked? We damn well ought to be shocked. If nobody is going to be shocked we might as well not tell them about it."[59] Sadly, rather than thinking deeply about how to best communicate the subversive truth about God's murder, some people today may obsess over Sayers's use of the word *damn*, considering it a betrayal of her Christian witness.

Such Christians need to know that even the word *atonement* was once considered a betrayal. Coined into English well over a millennium after Christ's resurrection, first as *"onement"* by John Wycliffe (1320s–1384), the term was handed over as *"atonement"* a century later in Tyndale's translation of the Bible. Constructed out of English words a preschooler would recognize—*at* and *one*—the new term implies that, by accepting the gift of forgiveness, we become *at one* with God and therefore start desiring what God desires for us: to follow the loving example of Jesus Christ. The word *atonement,* in other words, beautifully captures the essence of Christianity.

Nevertheless, both Wycliffe and Tyndale were persecuted for *atonement,* as for all English words in their Bible translations, because they had failed to use the traditional language of Christianity: Latin. Adding to the irony is the fact that the word *atone* has itself been reduced to an economy of exchange. Rather than thinking how it signifies Christ's gift of reconciliation, enabling us to become "at-one" with our Creator, people use it to reference something *they* have done: they have *atoned* for their sins through ritual, sacrament, devotion, or belief. Clearly, handing over a word or concept to new meanings can betray the faith all too quickly.

Maintaining the Foundational Essence of Christianity

Having been accused of betraying Christianity herself, Sayers repeatedly recommended books on Church history and theology, encouraging Christians to study the *essential* doctrines—the foundation of the house of Christianity—that were solidified at the First Council of Nicaea in 325; the First Council of Constantinople in 381; the Council of Ephesus in 431; and the Council of Chalcedon in 451. But why these four? After all, three more councils followed with proclamations of important doctrine. Sayers, like C. S. Lewis, emphasized the first four because they established fundamental doctrine that is still shared by believers from all three floors in the house of Christianity: Eastern Orthodox, Roman Catholic, and Protestant. Passionate about what she called the "Highest Common Factor of Consent" (rather than "lowest common denominator") among *all* Christians,[60] she echoed C. S. Lewis, who considered doctrine established at the first four Ecumenical Councils "mere Christianity."[61]

In fact, while Lewis was delivering his Broadcast Talks on BBC radio—the origin of his book *Mere Christianity*—Sayers was spearheading a project called "the Oecumenical Penguin" to publish, presumably with Penguin Books, the results of conversations among leaders from the three primary Christian traditions in England: Roman Catholic, Anglican, and Greek-Orthodox. Writing of her goals to the editor of *The Catholic Herald*, she explains that she wants to clarify what they all have in common, while "leaving out those points on which those bodies differ." And she identifies as their commonality "the doctrines accepted and defined at the Four Great Councils."[62] These doctrines, then, provide the unchanging "essence" of Christian tradition that is handed over to "new expressions" as culture changes.

For an analogy, readers might consider the US Constitution. The result of intelligent, sometimes heated, discussion among earnest leaders of a new "union" of states, the Constitution guides the law of the land. Nevertheless, sometimes its expression needs to be amended as culture changes, as when a Thirteenth Amendment was added to outlaw slavery. But that doesn't mean lawmakers abandoned the Constitution altogether: its essence persisted even as its expressions changed with culture. Furthermore, different political parties interpret how to uphold the Constitution differently, just as Roman Catholics and Protestants interpret how to uphold the Nicene Creed differently.

The big difference, of course, is that Christians believe that the Holy Spirit inspired the development of foundational doctrines of the faith, guiding church leaders in defining and refining the essential truths about God's entry into history. (Some believers, in fact, would say the same thing about the Constitution.) Nevertheless, while skeptics might consider such supernatural guidance a "quantum leap," well-informed Christians acknowledge the slow process of the Spirit's leading—like the movement of subatomic particles. Sayers, in fact, made this point to a Christian scientist: "If you follow out the history of the great dogmatic statements, you find that it is a history of successive revisions of the formula with a view to eliminating such possibilities of error."[63] This explains why it took nearly four and a half centuries before the essence of Christian doctrine was finalized.

A Concluding Betrayal

While some people uncritically celebrate change as progressive, others unquestioningly resist any kind of change, whether in belief or practice. Sayers, in contrast, would have us aim for a "delicate balance," preserving tradition by handing it over to new interpretations and meanings. Significantly, she used the term "delicate balance" with a close friend who had recently accepted the gift of salvation. Sayers's letter, written in joy, summarizes much that has been addressed in this chapter:

> The Event—the Act of God in History—is all-important because it ties the thing to this world, and to time and place and the flesh. . . . The event is susceptible of interpretation in all senses that don't contradict the central truth. . . . Hence the paramount importance of the central dogma. It doesn't, and it isn't supposed to, *exhaust* the meaning of the Event. But it's more like a set of pegs hammered in to prevent the whole fabric being wrenched out of shape in one direction or the other, through people getting too emphatic about one particular aspect of it. Hence heresies and other distortions,

which are *always* due to an over-simplifying emphasis of one truth at the expense of the others.[64]

Sayers would have us assess the legitimacy of changing interpretations of Christian practice by ascertaining whether they sustain or warp the tapestry of Christian dogma woven by Christian leaders in the early centuries of the Church.

Rather than being intimidated by changing interpretations of the truth, Sayers would have us celebrate the incarnation, which establishes that Jesus can speak to all times and in all places:

> God was also a man. And this particular Man it has never been possible to identify with any social, political, or economic system, or with any moral code. He seems literally all things to all men; to the rebel, a revolutionary; to the lover of political order, the sanction for the tribute paid to Caesar; to the virtuous, the King of virgins; to the sinner, the friend of harlots and publicans; to the pacifist, Prince of peace; to the warrior, a sword in the earth; to the gentle, meek and lowly, to the impatient, armed with vituperation and the scourge of small cords; to the light-hearted, the guest at Cana, to the melancholy, the Man of Sorrows; . . . to the humanist, perfect man, to the theologian, perfect God; filling all the categories and contained by none; and with all this, a single, recognizable, and complete Personality.[65]

The persisting essence of Christianity, of course, includes more than "this particular Man," the Son of God. There is a third person in the Trinity, whose nature was argued at the second Ecumenical Council, held at Constantinople in 381. This third member of the Trinity leads us to the next chapter. There we shall explore how Sayers not only maintained but also celebrated ancient doctrine by handing the Trinity over to new expressions of truth. For, as long as Christians walk this earth, there is no conclusion to the treason of tradition.

CHAPTER FOUR
THE SUBVERSIVE MIND OF THE MAKER

Rather than a mind for making money, Sayers had a mind for making change. Thus far we have focused on the *Why* of change, first in terms of Sayers's changing profession, both of her faith and in her career; next by considering her commitment to handing over truth. *Subversive* now turns to Sayers's sense of the *How*: the *practice* of making change, both for Christ and in culture.

The *How* of things was always very important to Sayers, perhaps explaining her success as an author of detective fiction. In her introduction to *Great Short Stories of Detection, Mystery, and Horror* (1929), she explains that, of the three questions key to solving a crime—Who? How? Why?—the *How* of mysterious action "offers most scope for surprise and ingenuity."[1] This chapter explores Sayers's insights about the subversive power of surprise and ingenuity: the *How* of Christian change. As always, be forewarned: Sayers tends to shock people by the way she maintains ancient truth by handing it over to new expressions.

A Zeal for Change

Sayers closes the play that changed her life, *The Zeal of Thy House,* with an angel praising the God of all creation: "Praise Him that He hath made man in His own image, a maker and craftsman like Himself."[2] These words are far more subversive than they may at first appear. Unlike Christians who seek to preserve the status quo or even return to the past, the angel's praise suggests that humans are most like God when they create something new.

Sayers bases this subversive idea on her interpretation of the *imago Dei*: Latin for "image of God." As recounted in the first chapter of the Bible,

> God created humankind in his image,
>> In the image of God [*imago Dei*] he created them;
>> Male and female he created them. (Genesis 1:27)

Sayers would then have us note the context in which the *imago Dei* is proclaimed: Genesis chapter one, which presents God not as lawgiver, not as judge, not as redeemer, but as creator. In fact, some scholars translate the self-describing term God gave to Moses from the burning bush as "I create what I create" (Exodus 3:14).[3] If humans are created in the image of God, then creativity must fulfill the *imago Dei*. It makes perfect sense.

But it is the *How* of this concept that shows Sayers's commitment to both creativity and Christ. For Sayers proceeds to suggest that creativity is trinitarian, like the God of Christianity. Reinforcing the belief that the universe was created by a Trinity, she has the angel at the end of *Zeal* pronounce that "every work of creation is threefold, an earthly trinity to match the heavenly."[4]

Sayers explains what she means by having the angel name the threefold work of human creativity *Creative Idea, Creative Energy,* and *Creative Power,* thus mirroring the three-in-one of Father, Son, and Holy Ghost.

It's easiest to understand what she means with the visual aid of a triangle. Just as a triangle has three angles in one form, so the Trinity has three persons in one substance, as in the diagram that follows.

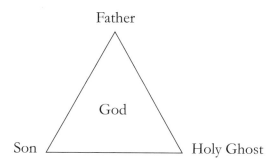

Mirroring this image is the second triangle below: *Idea* parallels the place of Father God; we see *Energy* at the Son of God angle; and at the Spirit's angle appears *Power.* In the center of the triangle is written *imago Dei.* In other words, the mind of the human maker mirrors the Mind of the Divine Maker.

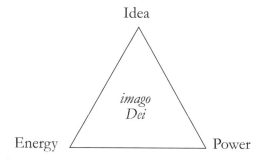

Professional theologians were amazed by Sayers's unusual—some would say subversive—insight. In fact, it was an influential British theologian who, after reading *The Zeal of Thy House*, suggested that Sayers expand on her trinitarian view of creativity. With his encouragement, she published a book-length study called *The Mind of the Maker* (1941), which outlines *how*, by paying attention to one's own creative process, a person can become aware of the three interdependent elements that are all part of any one creative project: a process that reinforces the essential doctrine, finalized centuries after the resurrection, that God, in whose image we are created, is three-in-one.

Creative Examples

For a simple, down-home example, think of a stay-at-home father who creates a healthy new recipe for his fussy children: first he has the Idea for a nutritious casserole they might eat, an Idea inseparable from the Energy manifest when he conceptualizes what ingredients he will use and then proceeds to mix the ingredients together. Power is manifest when the father tastes his own creation, perhaps making changes to guarantee it will entice his children. The three are all part of one work of creativity. (I give this example with a nod to Sayers's husband, who was the chef of their home, at least during the first decade of their marriage. When he published a *Gourmet's Book of Food and Drink* in 1935, he placed on his dedication page the words, "To My Wife, Who can make an Omelet.")

What Sayers made was books, not recipes. Hence, she explained her theology of creativity through what she knew best. For her, a creative project is composed of 1) *The Book as You Think*

It, which is the originating Idea; 2) *The Book as You Write It*, giving Energy to your Idea by incarnating it on the page; 3) *The Book as You and They Read It*, generating Power as you reread and revise, a Power that spreads as more and more readers respond to the spirit of your Idea incarnated through your words.[5] Sayers makes clear, however, that this does not imply a linear process. As with the Trinity, all three components are simultaneously part of the work, mutually interacting with one another in the act of creation. After all, as any creative writer will tell you, the Energy of writing down an Idea on the page makes it tangible, enabling the original Idea to expand its reach due to the Power generated when the author herself, by reading and revising her own incarnated Idea, actively develops it: the three are one during the act of creation.

Nevertheless, for both the chef and the author, creation is a step-by-step process, as illustrated by the Genesis account. After all, Omnipotent Triune God could have created everything in one Big Bang of glory. Instead, the opening chapter of the Bible emphasizes that creation happens over time, symbolically identifying each step with a new "day." The *imago Dei*, though three-in-one, also functions temporally.

While developing her theory about the *imago Dei*, Sayers was guided by the description of Christ at the start of John's Gospel: "All things came into being through him, and without him not one thing came into being" (1:3). Without the second Person of the Trinity, nothing comes into being. It reminds me of the many people I encountered in southern California who told me they had a great idea for a screenplay, as though to convince me of their creativity. But without giving Energy to their creative Ideas, they failed to bring their screenplays into being. And many screenplays that did come into being failed to generate the third component of the Creative Trinity: Power. Without the Power to attract any attention whatsoever, many screenplays languish in a drawer or on a thumb drive: an incomplete work of creation. Sayers therefore suggests two definitions of "work" in *The Mind of the Maker*: the action of work (creative working) and the work as a finished product of creativity.[6]

How, then, might *The Mind of the Maker* speak to those of us who are neither gourmet chefs nor bestselling authors? I can imagine two opposite reactions to Sayers's "curious" book, as she repeatedly called it. First are those who might humbly say, "I do not have a creative bone in my body; I can't cook up a new recipe, let alone write a screenplay." Second are those who might shout with excitement, "This is exactly what I believe! Christians need to support creative people who can communicate the Gospel message through the arts!" Sayers would respond to the first with encouragement, the second with caution.

A Zeal for Imagination: G. K. Chesterton

Without a doubt, works of imagination can change the way people think. Sayers would offer as examples authors who altered how she responded to Christianity. In 1954, when a distinguished scientist asked her about her faith, she explained the importance of G. K. Chesterton's creativity to her thought processes. Describing herself as "a sullenly unreceptive adolescent," not at all "religious by nature," Sayers states that she might well have turned into a Logical Positivist if not for Chesterton.[7]

Logical positivism broke onto the philosophical scene in the late 1920s, just as Sayers was establishing her reputation as creator of the decidedly non-Christian Peter Wimsey. Later called logical empiricism, logical positivism held that only empirically verifiable statements, along with logical proofs, can be considered true. This concept clearly dovetails with Sayers's creation of a sleuth who, like a scientist, looks to empirical evidence for clues about the truth. Fueling the idea that science and reason, rather than religion and faith, provide all the knowledge one needs in order to solve the mysteries of existence, logical positivism was attractive to Sayers during an era when she felt weighed down by Christian piety and propriety.

What kept Sayers from totally abandoning her faith, then, was the imaginative way Chesterton reframed Christianity. Attending guest lectures he delivered at Oxford University in 1914, Sayers had enjoyed the subversive quirkiness of Chesterton's book *Orthodoxy* (1908), which says things like, "The poet only asks to get his head into the heavens. It is the logician who seeks to get the heavens into his head. And it is his head that splits."[8]

Sayers clearly reflects the influence of Chesterton, when, decades later, she suggests that those who think science "almost infallible" have "completely lost touch with the whole field of poetic truth." Even more subversively, she proceeds to suggest that many evangelical Christians are merely the opposite side of the same "infallible" coin, demanding "literal belief in the historicity" of obviously poetic truths in the Bible.[9] Take, for example, adamant emphasis on a literal six-day creation. Christians who want the Bible to be scientifically accurate in every detail seem to suggest that only science delivers authentic truth; doing so, they imply that logical positivists are right: the Bible can't be true if it is not scientifically accurate. Sayers, in contrast, having learned from the subversive creativity of Chesterton, believed that God's revelation had higher truth claims than science. It is a revelation that gets our heads into the heavens often through "poetic truth," as in Christ's parables. At the same time, Sayers adamantly believed that the Bible reliably recounts the actual, historical death and resurrection of Jesus. Like Christ, who is the word of God, the Bible is both/and.

When Chesterton died in 1936, Sayers wrote his widow that "G. K.'s books have become more a part of my mental make-up than those of any writer you could name." And she makes clear that it wasn't simply *Orthodoxy* that kept her from giving up on orthodoxy, explaining the importance of Chesterton's novel *The Napoleon of Notting Hill*, which she read "at a very impressionable age."[10] Like Chesterton's other famous novels, especially *The Man Who Was Thursday* (1908) and *Manalive* (1912), *The Napoleon of Notting Hill* (1904) celebrates actions and activities that subvert cultural proprieties and pieties, his characters turning things upside down. In fact, sometimes Chesterton's protagonists turn themselves upside down quite literally, whether doing headstands and handstands or else hanging from tree limbs by their knees.

When her parents first recommended *Orthodoxy*, perhaps worried about the quirkiness of the Chesterton novels their daughter was reading, the fifteen-year-old Sayers responded with, "I am not surprised to hear that Chesterton is a Christian. I expect, though, that he is a very cheerful one, and rather original in his views, eh?"[11] The adjectives *cheerful* and *original,* followed by the tentative *"eh?,"* suggest her sense that Chesterton might be able to subversively turn upside down the dreary Christianity she had assimilated in her youth. Indeed, when the famous writer E. C. Bentley complimented Sayers on *The Zeal of Thy House,* she wrote back reporting the amusing irony that some critics considered her transition from detective fiction to religious drama subversively "indecent," following up by asking Bentley whether he noticed the "influence" of Chesterton on part of the play.[12]

A Zeal for Fantasy: C. S. Lewis

The creative work of Chesterton did for Sayers what the fiction of George MacDonald did for her friend C. S. Lewis. Though considering himself an atheist, the adolescent Lewis became powerfully intrigued by George MacDonald's Christian fantasy novel *Phantastes* (1858). It happened to him "almost unwillingly" as he puts it, having bought the novel in a train station only because he was desperate for something to read. As Lewis explains more than thirty years after the train ride, "the imaginative world of *Phantastes*" served to "convert, even to baptize . . . my imagination."[13] This does not mean that MacDonald's novel converted him to Christianity; Lewis didn't accept salvation through Christ until about sixteen years later. Nevertheless, MacDonald's fantasy world helped him imagine the universe in a whole new way, providing the light necessary to germinate a seed of faith.

Ironically, as Lewis explains in his introduction to *Phantastes*, "I should have been shocked in my 'teens if anyone had told me that what I learned to love in *Phantastes* was goodness."[14] Sayers would say the same thing about Chesterton. Though not an avowed atheist like Lewis, Sayers felt her faith was being choked by weeds of Christian legalism and hypocrisy, which made an atheistic philosophy like logical positivism seem enticingly attractive. For both Sayers and Lewis, then, it was imaginative creativity rather than rational apologetics that created in them new hearts: hearts open to belief in God-created "goodness."

And Sayers prophetically believed that Lewis would do the same for future generations. As she told a friend with young children, the Chronicles of Narnia reflect "the writer's very strong sense of the reality of good and evil," and she especially commends *The Silver Chair* and *The Voyage of the Dawn Treader*.[15] In an earlier letter to the same friend, in fact, Sayers comments that Lewis's best work is not to be found in his books about Christian apologetics, which appeal to reason, but in the Narnia tales, where not only does Christ appear as a "talking Lion," but "even the girls are allowed to take active part in adventures"—two different kinds of fantasy, at least in her era. Sayers also praises his science fiction novels (the Ransom trilogy), saying "Lewis has a remarkable gift for inventing imaginary worlds which are both beautiful and plausible—very unlike the dreary mechanisms of the space-fiction merchants."[16] She was most likely thinking of "the dreary" H. G. Wells, author of the famous science fiction novel *The War of the Worlds* (1898).

In 1947, Sayers received a letter from an Oxford University student asking her what he should read in order to resist the anti-Christian propaganda of H. G. Wells. She responded by expressing concern over the way Wells submitted to "the very common delusion that Science (in the modern sense) is able to deal not only with the *How* but with the *Why* of things." Describing Wells as "extremely brilliant," she suggests that his problem with Christianity probably results from warped views he internalized during childhood, describing them as "sketchy and inexact ideas picked up (poor man) in a dreadful little narrow sect in childhood and never corrected by the study of any modern or *imaginative* kind of theology."[17] Sayers's reference to "poor man" signals her ability to understand how some dreary brands of Christianity make scientific positivism seem highly attractive. The remedy, as Sayers herself discovered, is a more *imaginative* approach to theology, like that which she got from G. K. Chesterton. But rather than telling the Oxford student to read Chesterton as the best antidote to Wells, Sayers recommends C. S. Lewis, who creatively communicates the reality of good and evil.

A Zeal for Creation: J. R. R. Tolkien

Many today would say the same about the reality of good and evil communicated by Tolkien, whose creativity was valued by both Sayers and Lewis. Enamored of the good in Frodo and his elven friends, while disgusted with the selfish Sauron and the brutal orcs, readers have learned to love goodness through Tolkien, whose artistry has baptized their imaginations. But, as with the adolescent Lewis's response to MacDonald, that does not mean Tolkien's fiction converts readers to belief in Christ. It simply enables them to imagine a world in which the subversive nature of sacrificial love can save people from identifiable evil. To invoke Lewis's metaphor about MacDonald, baptism of the imagination, rather than brainwashing the intellect, removes the stain of incredulity that has obscured contemporary understandings of faith.

Like Lewis, Sayers would suggest that baptism of the imagination can wash away, or at least begin to dissolve, simplistic arguments that only scientifically verifiable, material realities can be true. Having felt the attraction of logical positivism, she would encourage us to support Christian fiction writers, as well as painters, musicians, filmmakers, and dancers, who can appeal to humanity's love for beauty and creativity. But she would also caution us, as would Tolkien. Committed, like Sayers, to fulfilling the *imago Dei*, Tolkien joyfully created another world for its own sake rather than as a means to present Christianity in new light. Instead of evangelism through the arts, he advocated "Sub-creation": authors created in God's image should create new worlds in their fiction.[18] As a result of this passionate belief, Tolkien thought that Lewis's Narnia stories were so obviously Christian in message that they were more like evangelistic allegory than authentically creative fiction.

The author of *The Lion, the Witch and the Wardrobe*, however, did not set out to write a Christian allegory in order to convert people. As is common for many creative writers, Lewis felt compelled by "a picture" that had entered his imagination: "a Faun carrying an umbrella and parcels in a snowy wood."[19] And he started writing a story around that image. Nevertheless, his Christianity shaped the narrative through his creation of a lion who dies to save others. In Sayers's terms, his Idea for a children's book about a faun carrying parcels took on Energy as he incarnated the Idea on paper—an incarnation, in his case, that literally entailed the incarnation of God in another world. As the Power of *The Lion, the Witch and the Wardrobe* spread to readers, it influenced Lewis as he developed the Idea for other Narnia Chronicles, each of which were incarnated on the page by the Energy of the word. Lewis, in fact, makes clear that he did not set out to write seven Narnia novels to fulfill some kind of pre-established schema.[20] Instead, Idea, Energy, and Power were mutually involved in each act of creation.

Though she loved Lewis's fiction, Sayers would understand Tolkien's hesitancy about the Narnia books. Sayers criticized Lewis's tendency "to think that one should rush into every fray and strike a blow for Christendom, whether or not one is equipped by training and temperament for that particular conflict," as she puts it to one correspondent. But then she adds that when Lewis is addressing an issue for which he is well equipped, "He is down on the thing like a rat; he is God's terrier, and I wouldn't be without him for the world."[21]

Sayers's assessment of Lewis goes back to her Bible-inspired belief that the Holy Spirit gives different gifts to different members of the body of Christ. As Paul implies to the Corinthians, an "ear" should not attempt to do the work of an "eye," nor an "eye" the work of "the hand" (I Corinthians 12:14–21). The creative work, in other words, functions best when the Power—which corresponds to the Holy Spirit in the *imago Dei* diagram—is fueled by the maker's Spirit-given gifts.

Christian Propaganda

Ironically, rather than celebrating gifts of creativity, many readers seem to prefer extracting propaganda or hidden agendas, even from Tolkien. In a letter Sayers wrote to Lewis soon after *The Fellowship of the Ring* was published (1955), Sayers compared the desire to draw culturally relevant messages out of Tolkien's novel with her parents' need to make sense of Chesterton's novel *The Napoleon of Notting Hill*. Their bafflement, in fact, may explain why they suggested she read Chesterton's *Orthodoxy*: a nonfiction work that "confused" them less than his strangely subversive novel.[22] Like Tolkien, however, Sayers valued creative work that ignites the imagination far more than books that overtly preach a message.

Sayers explicitly denounced the creation of literature simply to propagandize people—even with the Gospel message. Fiction written in order to "make the Christian Faith exciting" is, for her, "as corrupt as 'Fascist Mathematics' or 'Marxist Music,' or any other art or science that is harnessed to the service of an ideology."[23] When someone asked her opinion about the evangelistic possibilities of religious drama, she replied by emphasizing the need to place artistic quality first and foremost: "Piety and a spirit of prayer will not turn a bad play into a good one." No matter how sincere the intention that generated it or how orthodox the theology within it, "bad art is a thing damned in itself and damning in its effects."[24]

There are several reasons Sayers felt so passionately about this issue. First of all, evangelism through the arts can reek too much of an economy of exchange, turning creation into a utilitarian enterprise. As far as she was concerned, writing to generate converts, though noble in sentiment, is not that different in practice from writing to get wealth or fame in exchange. As she told one popular Christian writer, "You must not accept money, you must not accept applause, you must not accept a 'following,' you must not accept even the assurance that you're doing good as an excuse for writing anything but the thing you want to say."[25] And she assumes that what a Christian "wants to say," the Idea in the mind of the maker, is itself a gift from the Mind of the Maker in whose image we are created.

Significantly, Sayers wrote this exhortation to C. S. Lewis after she turned down his request to produce something for a series of books "on Christian knowledge" that might edify "young people" still in school.[26] He had written back, saying, "I wish I knew what place artistic consciences will hold a moment after death," as though God will judge her for turning down an opportunity to evangelize others.[27] However, having discovered in her first job out of university that she did not connect well with students, Sayers turned down the request for theological rather than "artistic" reasons.

She believed that God called her to use her creativity wisely, and because she could not do a good job with the assignment Lewis gave her, she preferred to concentrate on work she could do well.

This relates to the second reason Sayers denounced evangelism through the arts. As she told Lewis, "I don't believe God is such a twister as you make out." In other words, she didn't think God gave us particular gifts while expecting us to set them aside in order to evangelize others:

> I don't believe He implants a love of good workmanship merely as a trap for one to walk into. Of course one can make an idol of good workmanship, as of anything else. I don't know what will happen at the moment of death. But I don't somehow fancy showing . . . a lot of stuff to the Carpenter's Son and saying, "Well, I admit that the wood was green and the joints untrue and the glue bad, but it was all church furniture."[28]

Furniture can be "bad" in construction even when intended for "good" purposes. She acknowledges that "pious souls," welcoming anything with a Christian message, can "get comfort out of bad stained glass and sloppy hymns and music." But such souls seem to value the message more than the people it is supposed to attract—much as Christians valued King James English more than the people Sayers wanted to reach through *The Man Born to Be King*. Poorly crafted evangelistic art, as Sayers explains to Lewis, has caused "thousands" to think, "If Christianity fosters that kind of thing it must have a lie in its soul."[29]

In other words, bad art with an evangelistic message often pushes people away from Christ rather than drawing them closer. As Sayers tells her correspondent interested in evangelism through drama:

One of the most powerful arguments brought against the Church by intelligent people is the appalling corruption, not only of taste but of intellectual integrity, brought about by the sloppy music, ill-drawn and viciously coloured pictures and stained glass, degenerate third-hand architecture, and debased forms of pseudo-art in general that erupt all about her like maggots from a corpse.[30]

Incompetent art, even if intending to proclaim the glory of Christ's resurrection, will for many people leave Christ's body decaying in the tomb.

Sayers employed less subversive language in a lecture she delivered while *The Man Born to Be King* was halfway done with its original broadcast cycle. Arguing that "God is not served by technical incompetence," she tells of a Christian who asked her whether the actors playing angels in her play *The Zeal of Thy House* were chosen "for the excellence of their moral character." Sayers, of course, replied that their selection was based on the excellence of their craft, not their character. She fully believed that "the right kind of actor with no morals would give a far more reverent and seemly performance than a saintly actor with the wrong technical qualifications."[31] As far as she was concerned, those who do incompetent work while promoting Christian morals are turning their backs on the *imago Dei*.

A Zeal for the Gift of Creation

The opening chapter of the Bible suggests that creation is good in and of itself, rather than merely due to its utility, whether its usefulness is plants to eat, ticket sales to *Lord of the Rings* movies, or evangelizing students. After all, God did not *declare* each act of creation good due to its service to humanity; instead God "*saw*" that each creation was inherently good, the Hebrew word for *saw* repeated six times in one chapter: "And God saw that it was good."[32] Not coincidentally, Sayers inserts this repeated line from Genesis into her story about Jacob, the man born blind, in *The Man Born to Be King.* As we have seen, she has Jacob delight in the beauty of creation upon receiving his sight. After being reviled by religious authorities, Jacob is approached by Jesus a second time, as recounted in John 9. But then Sayers adds something not in John's Gospel: Jesus greets Jacob with these words: "And God looked at everything He had made, and behold! It was very good."[33] Jesus, in other words, did not heal Jacob in order to get something in exchange; instead, the healing was inherently good.

Sayers also believed that our own creations should not be exchangist—done solely to get something in return. Nevertheless, she also believed that the Power of a created work can be so transformative that it will bring people to faith: helping the blind to see. Though the work may generate fame and money, that's not why we choose to do it; we create because creation is good. We practice this truth any time we admire movies, paintings, architecture, and novels even when they are made by despicable people. Their creations can be good even when they aren't.

Sayers originally explored this insight in her script for *The Zeal of Thy House.* Whereas Adam and Eve fell because they wanted to be like God, the arrogant William of Sens actually believes that he is better than God, at least when it comes to the architecture of Canterbury Cathedral: "This church is mine / And none but I, not even God, can build it."[34] After he literally falls from scaffolding at the top of an arch, he slowly comes to the realization that arrogant pride is the chief of all sins. Nevertheless, even after he confesses his sin, he suggests that his creative work should not be judged by his own fallen, crippled nature:

> But let my work, all that was good in me,
> All that was God, stand up and live and grow.
> The work is sound, Lord God, no rottenness there—
> Only in me.[35]

William celebrates the *imago Dei*—his creativity—even as he confesses his fall into God-defying sin. Sayers thus makes the first three chapters of Genesis relevant not only to the twelfth century when William lived, but also to our own time, implying that the *imago Dei* and the Fall are simultaneously true: it's both/and.

Sayers also suggests that the *imago Dei* encompasses not only our being made in God's image, but also God's willingness to come to earth in *our* image to redeem us from consequences of the Fall; it's both/and. As she subversively puts it:

> For whatever reason God chose to make man as he is—
> limited and suffering and subject to sorrows and death—He
> had the honesty and the courage to take His own medicine.
> Whatever game He is playing with creation, He has kept
> His own rules and played fair. He can exact nothing from
> man that He has not exacted from Himself.[36]

As a result, even though we are sinners, we can fulfill the *imago Dei* through our creativity—not in exchange for our sins but as an inherent good that reflects the inherent goodness of our Creator.

Like Christianity itself, then, true creativity refuses an economy of exchange; it is a gift from God that one gifts to others. And because it is a gift, we need to be responsible not only in the way we exercise the gift, but also in how we welcome and receive gifts of creativity from others. This leads to how the *imago Dei* might function in those of us not called to be artists or bestselling authors.

Receiving Gifts of Creation

Sayers had plenty to say about the importance of creativity in those of us not gifted in the arts. After all, the way we respond to Shakespeare, Rembrandt, and Bach is essential to the third component of the creative Trinity: their Power. "Your response," she explains in *The Mind of the Maker*, "will bring forth further power, according to your own capacity and energy."[37] She gives concrete examples in a letter to a retired missionary, explaining how Christians can exercise the *imago Dei* through creativity *of judgment*. Renouncing complicity with the manufacture of embarrassingly tacky objects, followers of Jesus

> could refuse to buy sickly pictures and nauseating cards and calendars depicting limp Christs and anaemic angels; they could remove and bury beastly little statuettes of smirking Good Shepherds, and encourage little boys to have regrettable accidents with cricket-balls in the neighbourhood of the more offensive kind of stained glass windows.[38]

Rather than endorsing vandalism, Sayers is using hyperbole to shock her correspondent into new thought. Her words should make us think as well: how often do we drive people away from Christ by supporting tawdry Christian art?

But *how* do we know when art is tawdry? Sayers would answer, once again, with the need for education. In addition to studying

Church history and the "handing over" of tradition, she would have Christians study the history of art in order to understand the "handing over" of traditional styles. She wants us to know how to assess something as "good" rather than merely to base our judgments either on what we are used to (the status quo) or on what makes lots of money (an economy of exchange). To this end, Sayers describes in her letter to the missionary an incident when she complained in a shop about its "very twaddling Christmas stationery." The clerk could only tell her that, even though the store tries to stock more artistic merchandise, "the customers prefer this sort, and the clergy are the worst."[39] Shops carry tawdry art because it sells. This, of course, is nothing new. Even the word *tawdry,* a contraction of *St. Audrey,* reflects Christian practices. Referring to showy though poorly made lace collars called *St. Audrey's laces,* the word *tawdry* described products sold at medieval festivals celebrating St. Audrey, the patron saint of throat complaints. Economies of exchange have sullied Christianity in many different ways.

Sayers, then, would apply her same caution about buying tawdry Christian products to the way we buy into Tolkien, Lewis, and other successful Christian authors. As we respond to the Power of their fiction, we need to make sure that we are not motivated primarily by what *we get* in exchange. Sayers wrote a letter to Lewis about this very topic after a *Lord of the Rings* volume was reviewed in the *Times Literary Supplement* in December of 1955. She despairs how readers have done disservice to Tolkien's creativity by turning his novel into allegory: "If people are faced with an imaginative romance about a magic ring, they can't rest till they've reduced it to allegorical terms, and labelled and pigeon-holed everything for what it 'stands for.' The ring . . . has now been identified as Atomic, Political, and Bureaucratic power."[40]

The problem Sayers identifies arises because people want a return on their reading. Whereas some may argue that Tolkien meant the ring to represent Nazi power, other readers may impose a pre-established schema on the novels, such as hypothetically arguing that Tolkien intentionally aligned each of his four hobbit books with a different season of the year, even when there is plenty of evidence to suggest otherwise. As Sayers mentions in her letter to Lewis, critics who pick and choose passages that reinforce their interpretation often "make up imaginary biography to explain the bits they can't account for."[41] As far as she was concerned, such readings are far more about the cleverness of the critic than the goodness of the creation.

This does not mean that Sayers advocated a simplistic art-for-art's-sake response, one that worshipfully elevates the artist into a kind of priest who presents creative artifacts to venerate. Believing that Christian faith is always more important than the arts, Sayers wrote a letter to the editor of *The BBC Quarterly*:

> Enthusiasts need to be warned that aesthetic appreciation and emotional excitement are not substitutes for faith and works. . . . Experiencing a kind of internal oompah over the B Minor Mass [by Bach] is not the same thing as going to Mass; nor is the value of any devotional exercise to be measured by what you "get out of it," but by what you put into it.[42]

Aesthetic uplift, like religious emotion, can operate by an economy of exchange: valued only for what people get out of it.

Creative Heresies

Concerned about exchangist responses to art—from the idealizing of message to the idolizing of aesthetic emotion—Sayers spends a portion of *The Mind of the Maker* discussing imbalanced views of creativity. Just as many people ignore the equality of Father, Son, and Holy Spirit in the Trinity, so also many ignore the interaction among Idea, Energy, and Power in human creativity.

To address this imbalance, Sayers aligns self-serving responses to art with heresies that developed during the history of Christianity. For example, she parallels those primarily interested in message—like those people who argue that *The Lord of the Rings* is about atomic energy—with the heresy of the Manichees (her spelling), who considered spiritual knowledge good and material form evil.[43] In Sayers's terms, many readers, like writers themselves, become so obsessed with the message (Idea) a novel communicates that they ignore how it is incarnated on the page (its Energy). Rather than relishing imaginative plotting, consistency in characterization, and lucidly creative prose, such readers value Idea above everything else.

The opposite extreme Sayers calls "all technique and no vision," aligning this failure of creativity with the Arian heresy, which, as we have seen, used Scripture to argue that Jesus was not fully God.[44] Arius and his followers made the language (Energy) of Scripture more important than the Idea of the Trinity, much as Sayers's attackers in 1941 made the language of the King James Bible more important than the message (Idea) of the Gospels. Sayers argued, in contrast, that just as ancient doctrine reinforces that Father and Son were one at the moment of Creation (John 1:1–4), so also Idea and Energy in any creative work should be one. To emphasize one over the other is a heretical imbalance.

The hardest imbalance "to pin down" for Sayers is an overemphasis on Power, perhaps because most imbalanced readers (like viewers and listeners in the other arts) fall into one of the first two categories, either valuing message over technique or else so addicted to aesthetic stimulation that they pay no attention to ideas suggested by the work. For Sayers, Power must be creative in both maker and receiver. Makers need to look at their creations with critical eyes, thinking not just about form and content, but also about encouraging creativity in audience response. Writers and speakers insensitive to Power—power to ignite imagination— employ "worn-out metaphor and flowers of rhetoric trampled to death."[45] More often than not, they do so because their listeners, readers, and viewers prefer the comfort of predictable clichés to the subversive Power of creativity, much as the consumers excoriated by Sayers prefer "sickly pictures and nauseating cards." Rather than valuing something that challenges both thought and imagination, whether coming from the pulpit, podium, stage, or screen, such consumers want products that either reinforce their worldview on the one hand, or else generate mindless stimulation on the other.

Good Work Well Done—or Not

This brings us to one of Sayers's most subversive statements: "*The only Christian work* is good work well done . . . whether it is church embroidery or sewage farming."[46] Here we see Sayers's emphasis that creativity, and hence the *imago Dei*, is not solely about making an artifact to be read, heard, or viewed with delighted admiration, as her shocking reference to sewage farming implies. Indeed, Sayers would respond to any Christian who bemoans, "I do not have a creative bone in my body" with the fact that many a book has been published that does not have a creative bone in *its* body. As she tells one correspondent, "The shelves of the British Museum groan under accumulations of dry, stupid, and trivial books, the whole of whose verbiage is not worth ten syllables of one of Shakespeare's Sonnets, or a single saying of Jesus."[47] Unlike dry, stupid, and trivial books, creativity has to do with something new, echoing the creations of God. Scores and scores of books, including books by Christians, merely repeat what has already been made clear in multiple previous publications. By failing to acknowledge or even acquaint themselves with the creativity of their predecessors, what Sayers calls "former streams of beauty, emotion, and reflection,"[48] the authors of such books do dishonor to the *imago Dei* in those that came before them—as well as in themselves. The sewage farmer, by researching new ways to use her product for fertilizer even as she works to reduce its smell, may be doing far more creative work.

Many people, of course, do not have the opportunity to be creative at their jobs. Instead, they manifest the *imago Dei* in other areas of their lives, through creative family functions, hobbies, or community engagement. For many, such activities bring them great joy, thus fulfilling Sayers's insight that good work well done "is not, primarily, a thing one does to live, but the thing one lives to do."[49] In other words, good work well done, though often money-making, is not *primarily* motivated by an economy of exchange.

In this light, Sayers helps us see, once again, the profundity of Christ's comment that "it is easier for a camel to go through the eye of a needle than for someone who is rich to enter the kingdom of heaven" (Matthew 19:24). A man who can buy anything he wants doesn't have to be creative; he can simply pay others for their creativity. His commitment to an economy of exchange outweighs his commitment to fulfill the *imago Dei*.

Disgusted by the "greed and waste which we dignify by the name of a 'high standard of living,'"[50] Sayers would challenge the wealthy to be genuinely creative about the way they spend both money and time: creating and sustaining funds for needy causes rather than for self-glorification; producing insightful, creative films rather than merely investing in money-generating or propagandistic movies; encouraging the *imago Dei* in their children rather than simply paying and paving their way into the most prestigious schools and expensive programs. In other words, creative philanthropists operate according to the concept of the gift—the distinguishing mark of Christianity—rather than exchange. After all, Sayers suggests, any conformist nincompoop (a word she uses several times in her letters) can buy commodities for friends and family, passively responding to all those "advertisements imploring and exhorting and cajoling and menacing and bullying us to glut ourselves with things we did not want, in the name of snobbery and idleness and sex appeal."[51] But a millionaire who provides for strangers in a way that creatively energizes their lives is doing "good work well done."

Sayers does not let the less-than-wealthy off the hook, either. In her essay on the deadly sins she asks:

Do we admire and envy rich people because they are rich, or because the work by which they made their money is good work? . . . When we invest our money, do we ask ourselves whether the enterprise represents anything useful, or merely whether it is a safe thing that returns a good dividend?[52]

These questions amplify her rendition of Christ's "eye of the needle" statement in *The Man Born to Be King*: "it is easier for a camel to go through the eye of a needle than for those that set store by riches to enter the kingdom God."[53] In other words, anyone can "set store by riches" as much as (if not more than) the wealthy do. Sayers would rather that we all set store by the *imago Dei*.

Sayers summarizes her challenge in a lecture she delivered a year after the publication of *The Mind of the Maker*. Calling it "Why Work?," Sayers exhorts her listeners to aim for "creative activity undertaken for the love of the work itself." Clearly, she believes that humans, "made in God's image, should make things, as God makes them."[54] A natural question arises from her exhortation: how might those of us with limited resources and meager talents "make things"? Sayers, in addition to telling us the answer, exemplifies it: we can fulfill the *imago Dei* through the way we *make meaning*. The work of language can *create* new insight.

A Talent for Words

We have seen that Sayers transformed a nation through the unusual language she employed in the BBC radio plays about Jesus, drawing thousands to take the Gospel message seriously. Even the word *Trinity*, which inspired her view of the *imago Dei*, was once a new creation. Because *Trinity* appears nowhere in Scripture, a theologian named Tertullian felt the need (around 200 CE) to *make* a word that might capture a concept suggested by the Bible. Inspired by the Idea of a three-in-one God, which had been explored by earlier theologians, Tertullian gave Energy to the Idea by coining the term *Trinitas* in Latin. And the Power of this word has shaped Christian thought ever since. Once again, however, this does not mean that the *imago Dei* can only be fulfilled by brilliant theologians like Tertullian and talented authors like Sayers, Lewis, and Tolkien. The word *talent* can apply to us all.

Talent comes from a biblical sign for money; in first-century Palestine a talent was worth about one hundred denarii. As Christ's Parable of the Talents makes clear (Matthew 25:14–30), not everyone is given the same talents. The Master in the story gives one servant five talents, another two, the third servant only one, "each according to his ability." While the first two servants invest their talents and multiply them, the third protects his talent by burying it, causing the Master to reprimand him.

Though some people pull the parable out of context to use as an endorsement of capitalism, Matthew embeds the story among several parables critiquing the lack of creative action. Rather than endorsing an economy of exchange, the stories address people's failure to use the resources they have been given, either by birth or by circumstances. It is therefore no coincidence that, by the thirteenth century, the word *talent* had taken on the meaning we use today. And though some extraordinary people like Sayers, Tolkien, and Lewis were given five talents, all of us have been given at least one: a talent for communication. We therefore need to ask ourselves whether we bury our talent for communication or make it multiply through creative use of language. As Sayers points out to the secretary of Oxford University's Socratic Club, "Poetical use of Language is not confined to 'Literature,' but occurs also and most notably, in common speech."[55] Knowing that the word *poet* comes from the Greek word for *maker*, she suggests that all forms of communication have the potential to reflect the *imago Dei*.

Take, for example, evidence provided by my friend Carole, who witnessed the creative use of language in her work as a deaf education specialist. Her students would often come up with their own creative signs, thus distinguishing their communication from the authorized version of sign language—much as Sayers distinguished her communication of the Gospel message from the Authorized Version of the Bible. The creation of new signs—whether spoken with the tongue, written on a computer screen with thumbs and fingers, or signed with hands and arms—can change the way people think, including the way people think about Christ.

In *The Mind of the Maker,* Sayers explicitly states that "common" people are more aligned with artists than people in any other profession, since God calls both to manifest "that image of the Creator which distinguishes the man from the beast."[56] Indeed, while some apes have been taught by human trainers to use sign language, it always seems to be in the context of exchange: the apes mimic certain signs that will get them food or attention in return. Humans have a very different gift, which became clear to me when a graduate student. While taking a city bus on the way to class, frantically trying to finish assigned reading, I overheard a conversation among some fellow passengers who were questioning a statement that had confused them. One finally pronounced, "Sometimes words gotta do strange things in order to mean anything." It was the most insightful comment I heard or read all day.

Unfortunately, most people don't think about the Power of words, merely using conventional, generic language to get something they want, whether that's getting people to agree with them, to sleep with them, or to pass the potatoes: language as a form of exchange. In contrast, creative Christians, fulfilling the *imago Dei,* use their God-given brains both to create new ideas and to express old ideas in new ways. As Sayers sees it, "Words are actually a kind of high explosive" that can clear away centuries of exchangist thought.[57] She so believed in the Power of new words that she feared her unusual language in *The Man Born to Be King* would lose its explosive quality if the plays were re-broadcast too often. Like organ music in church, her radio scripts would simply become the new status quo: comforting in their familiarity. Sometimes words gotta do strange things in order to mean anything.

Signs of New Life

Sayers considered Jesus, the word of God, the perfect model for language explosive enough to bring down tiresome religious clichés. Just think of the way Jesus subversively shocked Nicodemus into a new way of thought. Approaching Jesus under the cover of darkness, Nicodemus told the subversive teacher that his miracles showed God was "with him." Jesus responded by giving Nicodemus not a miracle but a different kind of language: "Except a man be born again, he cannot see the kingdom of God." The metaphor was so unusual that Nicodemus protested: "How can a man be born when he is old? Can he enter his mother's womb a second time and be born?" (John 3:2–4, KJV). I quote from the King James Version to highlight the irony of protests over *The Man Born to Be King*: Christians wanted to hold onto traditional language about a Christ who challenged traditional language.

Sayers puts Nicodemus into her radio plays, establishing that his character was drawn to Jesus while also being concerned about precision in language. Joining Caiaphas and others at the trial of Jesus, Sayers's Nicodemus tries to find a loophole in accusations against Jesus: "Did he say he would destroy [the Temple], or only that he could?" Unfortunately, Nicodemus ultimately sides with the religious status quo. Describing his character in notes for the plays, Sayers states that Nicodemus, despite his "convictions," is too timid "to defy authority."[58] Nicodemus is thus the mirror opposite of Sayers's Judas. Disgusted with people in authority, Judas trusts his certitude more than Jesus, whereas the very uncertain Nicodemus trusts people in authority more than Jesus. Though opposites, both serve the interests of Caiaphas, who enables the Romans to kill Christ. Not coincidentally, Sayers has Jesus tell Judas the story of Nicodemus questioning "born again."

Rather than imitating either Judas or Nicodemus, Sayers would have us exercise the *imago Dei*, taking advantage of what she calls, in *The Mind of the Maker*, "the metaphorical nature of all language."[59] Creative metaphors, by drawing new pictures in people's minds, can subvert resistance to ideas that have annoyed if not disgusted people in the past. Christ's parables, for example, reflect the subversive mind of the maker. Even many non-Christians use the term *good Samaritan* to describe a certain kind of selfless hero. This often happens to creative language; igniting thought, it spreads like fire as people spark each other's imaginations.

Problematically, creative language that once spread like wildfire can leave scorched earth behind, inhibiting new growth. Here's an example from my own life that I wrote up in another book. Relevant to *The Mind of the Maker*, it bears repeating:

> Several Christmases ago, . . . my brother-in-law found himself in a long line at the post office. Watching tinsel trickle down from evergreen boughs over the windows, he (like everyone else in line) overheard a loud conversation between two package-toting customers complaining about their in-laws. Each trying to trump the other with

a story of in-law dysfunction, one finally said, "and then she became a *born-again Christian*." Ten people standing in line all groaned in unison.[60]

Rather than groaning at overheard tales of in-law flatulence and sibling nose-picking, they groaned over the words "born again." When I consulted evangelical pastors about this incident, they agreed that the term *born-again Christian* seems to repel more than compel, pushing people away from the truth of Christ rather than igniting new thought. This is because, all too often, people who use that identifier act like the Christians who outraged Sayers, elevating piety, prosperity, and/or politics over the subversive nature of God's love.

Nevertheless, some will insist on continuing to use *born again* due to the fact that Jesus coined it. There are several ironies here. First, as more recent translations of John's Gospel suggest, Jesus said "born from above," not "born again." But even though Jesus did creatively imply the idea of being "born again," those who insist on using the term often ignore other things Jesus said, like John 13:14: "So if I, your Lord and Teacher, have washed your feet, you also ought to wash one another's feet." Picking and choosing Bible passages to conserve the way they have always been taught, such Christians worship words of the past more than the living word of God, committing what Sayers calls a "singular piece of idolatry."[61] In contrast, Jesus transformed the world with new signs and wonders: not only miracles, but also the signs and wonders of language. If, indeed, "born again" has become what Sayers calls a "worn-out metaphor," deadening people to life in Christ, how might we communicate Christian truth with new language?

Subversive Creativity

Let me give another example from my own life. I had recently started a new teaching job at a Christian college, where I was excited about integrating my faith with my scholarship. Early in the semester, I went to a chapel service to hear one of my colleagues give the morning homily. When he mentioned an incident in which a Mennonite man of God was asked, "Are you a Christian?" I immediately thought about how I had been trained to answer the question: "I was born again when I asked Jesus into my heart at age eight." But then my colleague went on to say, "The man of God answered the question 'Are you a Christian?' with 'Ask my neighbor.'" I nearly fell off the folding chair, overwhelmed with the impact of such language. If my neighbor sees no difference in my life—a difference that attracts rather than repels—what is the point of having Jesus "in my heart"? Is my "personal relationship with Jesus" merely "personal" fire insurance, guaranteeing that I don't go to hell? I was immediately struck by the hypocrisy of my ingrained prejudice against Roman Catholics, whom I had considered idolaters due to statues of Mary in their churches. At that very moment I recognized my idolatry of words, believing that only certain language could be offered up in exchange for salvation.

Something similar happened when I started studying the work of Sayers. Knowing she was an important influence on C. S. Lewis, I kept being shocked by the subversive way she put things, as when she told one correspondent, "In order that you may freely choose God, you must also be free to reject Him; you may say that God was ready to die—and in fact He did die—for your right to blaspheme Him if you choose."[62] Such a shocking idea forced me to see God's amazing sacrifice as though with a search-light, rather than merely with the muted light that shines through stained-glass depictions of a calm and tidy crucifixion.

Sayers wrote subversive words because Jesus, the word of God in whose image she was created, was subversive:

> He drove a coach-and-horses through a number of sacrosanct and horary regulations; He cured diseases by any means that came handy, with a shocking casualness in the matter of other people's pigs and property; He showed no proper deference for wealth or position; when confronted with neat dialectical traps, He displayed a paradoxical humor that affronted serious-minded people, and He retorted by asking disagreeably searching questions that could not be answered by rule of thumb.[63]

Following Christ's example, she wrote subversive words in reaction to the many "serious-minded" believers who end up repelling rather than compelling belief:

> Somehow or other, and with the best intentions, we have shown the world the typical Christian in the likeness of a crashing and ill-natured bore—and this in the Name of One who assuredly never bored a soul in those thirty-three years during which He passed through this world like a flame.[64]

Through her creative use of language, Sayers helped me see God as a subversive Creator, one who desires to make all things new, rather than merely "as an elderly invalid who might collapse from shock if suddenly intruded on by a common person bouncing in."[65] Created in God's image, we are encouraged to go and do likewise.

Some readers may feel exhausted right now, thinking, "How can I possibly come up with creative new language all the time?" That is a valid question, and Sayers would quite rightly answer that it's not necessary all the time or even most of the time. And she might justify her response with a famous statement by the Roman orator Quintilian, at least as translated by eighteenth-century British pundit Samuel Johnson: "Language is the dress of thought."

Changing the Dress of Thought

When Sayers wanted to change the way her culture thought about women, she suggested that women be allowed to change the way they dressed. In both "Are Women Human?" (1938) and "The Human-Not-Quite-Human" (1941), she argues that women should be allowed to wear trousers: an idea she recognizes as "distressing" to religious leaders in her day. Responding to those who assert trousers "are extremely unbecoming," she suggests that culturally constructed concepts of what is "unbecoming" often prevent women from *becoming* human: "As a human being, I like comfort and dislike draughts. If the trousers do not attract you, so much the worse; for the moment I do not want to attract you. I want to enjoy myself as a human being."[66] Sayers recognized that in some contexts skirts may be more appropriate than trousers; she did not proclaim a need to replace one's entire wardrobe. And she would assert the same about the dress of thought.

Just as we don't go out and buy a new outfit every time we get dressed, so also we don't dress our thoughts with new expressions every time we speak. Language, like clothing, is a basic necessity for daily existence. Only for special occasions do we clothe our bodies with something entirely new in order to communicate appreciation, respect, and/or excitement for an event. Similarly, only on special occasions should we use new language to communicate appreciation, respect, and excitement for God's Gift. As Sayers explains to C. S. Lewis:

> You must speak to and for your audience. . . . But you must not tell people what they want to hear, or even what they need to hear, unless it is the things you passionately want to tell them. You must not look at them from above, or outside, and say: "Poor creature; they would obviously be the better for so-and-so—I must try and make up a dose for them."[67]

By "make up a dose for them," Sayers suggests a problem with a lot of evangelistic language: it seems offered only as a take-this-because-it's-good-for-you tonic. Often concocted from familiar clichés and same-old, same-old God-talk, it leaves a very bad taste—as exemplified by the people who responded to "born again" in the post office.

Nevertheless, Sayers would find it a bit ironic that many Christians are willing to spend hours, if not days, shopping for a new item of clothing or a new car, but spend little time thinking about how to dress their thoughts with new language, or how to turn the ignition switch on a new vehicle of thought. Because creative language can transport skeptics to a new place of faith, Sayers believed that Christians should be willing to spend as much time thinking about how to communicate the significance of God's Gift as they do purchasing vehicles and clothes. Sometimes arguing with her husband about who got to drive their motorcycle and who had to sit in the sidecar, Sayers wanted Christians to communicate as much excitement about their faith as she did about the family motorcycle:

You've got to come galloping out shouting excitedly: "Look here! Look what I've found! Come and have a bit of it—it's grand—you'll love it—I can't keep it to myself, and anyhow, I want to know what you think of it." Then it's all jam, and the thing will go round and multiply, like the loaves and fishes or the water made wine.[68]

The signs and wonders of language can help others see that the bread of life and the wine of salvation are miraculous gifts.

Signs and Wonders of Language

Significantly, every time Gospel writers talk about "signs," as in "signs and wonders," they employ the Greek *semeion*, which means "sign." This Greek word is the source of our word *semantics*, which refers to how language makes meaning. Many of us have heard the phrase "It's only a matter of semantics," often said dismissively. Sayers would retort that creative language *is* a matter of semantics! By creating new signs to communicate old meanings, our language can change lives.

Think about the first chapter of Genesis, which describes God *speaking* the universe into existence: "And God *said* 'Let there be light' . . . And God *said* . . . Then God *said*"—nine times in one chapter. This helps explain the start of John's Gospel: "In the beginning was the Word, and the Word was with God, and Word was God. He was in the beginning with God. All things came into being through him." In Sayers's terms, God's Creative Idea is inseparable from the Energy of God's Creative Word: the Son, Jesus Christ, who, with God at the moment of creation, generated the Power of light: "Let there be light" (Genesis 1:3). Only twenty-three verses later we read, "Let us make humankind in our image, according to our likeness." The *imago Dei,* then, celebrates speaking the new into existence, as when Sayers brought newness of life to thousands of people by creating subversively original words in her BBC radio plays. Let there be light!

In this light (as it were), it might be instructive to think once again of the miraculous way Jesus brought light to the blind. While he puts clay on the eyes of the man born blind and then directs him to wash in the Pool of Siloam, others he simply touches with his hands or says a word and they are made whole. He actually leads one blind man out of town and then spits in his eyes. It clearly would have been far more efficient to use the same technique for every blind person, freeing up time for Jesus to do more signs and wonders. But the creative work of healing, like God's own self, is trinitarian: the Idea of giving sight is inseparable from the Energy of act and word, both of which are inseparable from the Power on the blind person. Jesus, it would seem, knew that Power breaks through blindness differently with different people. In other words, rather than protecting his busy schedule or preserving traditional practices, Jesus responded to the needs of individuals.

The same might be said about our fulfillment of the *imago Dei* through creative use of language. A semantic approach that might help one spiritually blind person finally *see* Jesus may be considerably different from the way another person finally understands the gift Christ has offered. Sayers confirms this concept in a letter to someone grappling with what it means to become a Christian:

> Some people want to find something that makes sense of history, or of the cosmic set-up; others are bothered about the

value of suffering; others start off from a strong sense of sin (I mean, of something fundamentally wrong about themselves and humanity in general); others from seeing how the patterns of all religions are actualised in the Christian pattern—it's just a question of going whichever way seems the right way for you, because any road is right if it gets there.[69]

By "any road" she does not mean any religion, as should be very clear by now. Instead, it's about following the example of Jesus, who was sensitive to the differing needs of individual seekers rather than worried about his efficiency as a healer of spiritual blindness.

Creative Examples

How, then, do we dress our thought in such a way that people might see the profundity of ancient Christian doctrine in a new light? Sayers would have us create metaphors based on our own life experiences, and thus exemplify the mind of the maker: "an Idea in your mind, the manifestation of that Idea in some form of Energy or Activity (speech, behavior, or what not), and a communication of Power to the world about you."[70] Because Energy in her trinitarian concept correlates with incarnation, creative metaphors about life often arise from one's own embodied (incarnated) experiences. As Sayers puts it, "You've got to begin with something known and concrete, like buttons or cats, otherwise it all seems like a bandying of words without relevance to reality."[71]

For example, in order to explain life apart from God, a swimmer might talk about failing to get close enough to the pool wall to make the turn during a race: a failure that makes her dead in the water. A pianist might talk about sitting down at a recital only to discover that the people supplying the instrument had failed to tune it, making all his skill and practice futile. Many of us can talk about discovering a cell phone dead right when we needed it to address a crisis. These examples, of course, are just starts to metaphors, but they illustrate, if even inadequately, how new language might ignite conversation rather than generate groans while in line at the post office.

And Sayers serves as a fantastic mentor. Almost every quotation of hers in this book employs everyday words that most English speakers would understand. It's the way she creatively puts the words together, like buttons and cats, that makes the difference. As she explains to one correspondent, "What I say is what the Church says—only the language is different." And she practices what she preaches to another correspondent, asserting that the gospel she offers "differs from the regulation diet in nothing but in being served up in plain English and without slop-sauce or sectarian skewers."[72] As far as she was concerned, then, if terms like *born again* or *evangelical* have become distasteful slop-sauce for numerous skeptics, turning them away from God, those terms should be taken off the menu. Failure to do so becomes idolatry: a worship of words more than love for the Word who transcends all language.

A commitment to new language is especially important to the next chapter, which is going to make some people angry. That is because it is about politics: always a touchy subject. Sayers, I hope to show, can guide us through the trenches of contemporary culture, where many of us feel overwhelmed and underdressed as we face bombardment by weaponized words. Like the apostle Paul, who came up with a creative metaphor for handling assaults in his own day—"Put on the whole armor of God" (Ephesians 6:11)—Sayers will hand us new clothing of thought, enabling us to creatively celebrate the Mind of our Maker in the midst of vicious attacks from both the right and the left.

CHAPTER FIVE
THE POLITICS OF RELIGION, THE RELIGION OF POLITICS

It was politics that got Jesus crucified. And politics continue to crucify the truth.

Sayers made this point not long after *The Zeal of Thy House* transformed her life. In a 1938 article for the *Sunday Times*, she proclaimed that "God was executed for being a political nuisance, *'under Pontius Pilate'*—much as we might say, 'when Mr. Joynson-Hicks was Home Secretary.'"[1] Sayers's political allusion is revelatory. In 1924, William Joynson-Hicks became Home Secretary for the United Kingdom (comparable to the US Secretary of State), and developed a reputation for being "the most prudish, puritanical, and protestant Home Secretary of the twentieth century."[2] Taking a self-righteous stand against drinking after hours as well as literary allusions to sex, Joynson-Hicks would have considered Jesus, who spent time with winebibbers and sinners, to be a political nuisance who enjoyed subverting the status quo. As Sayers goes on to say, after alluding to Joynson-Hicks, "leading authorities in Church and State considered that [Jesus] talked too much and uttered too many disconcerting truths."[3]

When Sayers began to conceptualize her scripts for *The Man Born to Be King* two years later, she made politics essential to retelling the story of God's murder. While composing the first play about Herod's decision to kill all infants in order to get rid of the one worshipped by Magi, she wrote to a BBC producer, saying, "It's important that this shouldn't be looked on as a mere piece of meaningless savagery. It was a perfectly reasonable *political* step, if you once allow that the good of the State is more important than the rights of the individual."[4] Politicians like Herod, in other words, want to eliminate programs and persons who might upset the smooth running of the state. This helps explain why the BBC radio broadcasts led scores of people to take Jesus seriously for the first time in their lives: the Gospel suddenly seemed relevant to existence as they knew it. Unlike sanitized depictions frozen in stained-glass windows, Sayers's Bible characters encountered many of the same frustrations, the same joys, and the same political maneuverings as people living nearly two thousand years later.

This, of course, was Sayers's point. As she explains in her introduction to the 1943 print version of the twelve scripts,

> God was executed by people painfully like us, in a society very similar to our own—in the over-ripeness of the most splendid and sophisticated Empire the world has ever seen. In a nation famous for its religious genius and under a government renowned for its efficiency, He was executed by a corrupt church, a timid politician, and a fickle proletariat led by professional agitators.[5]

Sayers wrote these words in the middle of World War II, when Britain was still an imperial power with multiple colonies. After the war, of course, the United States began emerging as "the most splendid and sophisticated Empire the world has ever seen," making Sayers's comment seem especially relevant to the over-ripeness of America today. Sayers can help disaffected believers (and, with God's grace, even the Christians who anger them) grapple with political antagonisms that wrack multiple nations—and murder truth in the process.

I must warn you, however: Sayers's belief that ancient Christian Creeds speak to traditional party politics will make many people angry—as happened in her own day. When she gave lectures on the radio about the relationship between Christ and culture, she got letters from "a more than usually fruity crop of candidates for the loony bin!"[6] As far as she was concerned, candidates for the loony bin are people who unthinkingly denounce, usually with a sneer, any idea that challenges their political and/or religious beliefs. Sayers would rather have all of us cultivate the fruits of the Spirit as we respond to our increasingly polarized culture.

Political Activism and Religion

While writing *The Man Born to Be King*, Sayers constructed an antagonism between opposing political interests that is still relevant today: progressives, who want to institute original new programs, versus traditionalists, who want to maintain (or reinstate) ideas and practices that were valued in the past. Rather than endorsing one side over the other, however, Sayers challenges true believers from both the right and the left, encouraging all to assess how their rhetoric muffles the subversive words of Jesus.

The radicals of Christ's day were called Zealots, and Sayers makes them essential to the plotting of her radio plays. Because the Bible makes only brief mention of "Simon the Zealot" (Luke 6:15 and Acts 1:13), Sayers read scholarly histories on classical Roman culture in order to learn more about how the Zealot nationalist party operated during the time of Jesus. She quotes scholar A. H. M. Jones in the notes for her fourth radio play: "The Zealots rejected the opportunist fatalism of the conservative Pharisees; God, they declared, would help only those who helped themselves, and it was the duty of every Jew to fight for national independence."[7] Jewish Zealots resented taxes imposed by their Roman oppressors, taxes that often went into the coffers of those with power rather than being spent to improve life for average Jewish citizens. It is no wonder that Jesus was denounced for socializing with tax collectors!

Sayers goes into detail about the Zealots in order to establish background for one of the most important fictional characters she inserts into *The Man Born to Be King*: Baruch the Zealot. Because Sayers subverted traditional views of Judas, as discussed in chapter 3, she needed to create a narrative device that explains why Judas ended up betraying Jesus. Baruch provides that motivation, eventually convincing the most passionately committed disciple that Jesus cannot be trusted. As Sayers explains in her introduction to the printed plays, Baruch's "connection with Judas supplies the main-spring of the plot-machinery."[8]

The radical Baruch serves more than plot-machinery, however. Sayers gives him dialogue that sounds very much like political party operatives, not only in her day but also in our own. In her fifth play, Baruch says, "The party is ready. . . . All we need is a figurehead, a leader, a spell-binder to fire the imagination of the masses and make them fall in to march behind the party. . . . Brains aren't enough. You've got to appeal to the emotions."[9] Not surprisingly, Baruch thinks that a street preacher named Jesus bar-Joseph might fit the bill. After all, Jesus was drawing crowds to rally-like sermons while repeatedly criticizing conservative religious leaders who wanted to protect the status quo rather than transform lives. This explains why Baruch, unbeknownst to Judas, sends Jesus a note outlining the possibilities for a triumphal entry into Jerusalem: if Jesus rides a horse into the city a group of Zealots will follow, rushing in to ignite a revolution. Jesus, of course, repudiated a political revolution by choosing a lowly donkey for his entry.

Sayers also shows that, like a true politico, Baruch denounces the opposition: those who support the Roman rule of Caesar because it serves their own best interests. As Baruch puts it, "Caesar preaches another kind of salvation—prosperity, security, the world-wide peace of Rome. 'Order and safety'—that is their motto. . . . And so they dope the masses with propaganda, while we that have heart and spirit to fight are kept quarrelling among ourselves."[10] One need only access any newsfeed during an election cycle to see the relevance of Baruch's comments to our own day, when politicians manipulate religious voters by promising prosperity, order, and safety—even though such promises run counter to Christ's teachings.

However, this does not mean that Sayers considered progressive radicals (at least once they stop "quarreling") as God's answer to all political ills. In her quotation of historian A. H. M. Jones, she highlights a problem with the Zealots: "The party developed into a powerful secret organisation which waged an unrelenting campaign of assassination and terrorism, directed as much against the loyal Jews, whom they regarded as traitors to *the national cause*, as against the Roman government."[11] Nationalism, as Sayers makes clear repeatedly during *The Man Born to Be King*, can lead to vile policies and practices—whether implemented by ideologues on the right or the left.

Nationalism versus Patriotism

Nationalism is not the same thing as patriotism. Sayers herself was extremely patriotic. As Barbara Reynolds notes in her biography of Sayers, the woman's "sense of responsibility" to her country was "titanic" during World War II: "She took part in conferences, she gave talks to the Forces, she broadcast, she wrote letters to the press, she wrote articles, she formed a group for knitting socks and sweaters, . . . she became an air-raid warden and took her share of fire-watching."[12] Rather than being nationalistic, Sayers's energetic patriotism was *in reaction to* nationalism: German nationalism, whereby Hitler galvanized a whole country through highly charged political rhetoric, justifying the extermination of millions with promises to return the country to its former glory. Setting up the nation as an idol, nationalists seek to sweep the country clean of any human who doesn't fit their requirements for purity, whether ethnic, racial, sexual, or political. Indeed, many people forget that Hitler worked to eliminate not only Jews, Romani, and homosexuals, but also Aryans who had disabilities—including children. Furthermore, when military and party leaders questioned Hitler's tactics, they were ousted from their jobs and often imprisoned.

Not coincidentally, then, Sayers explicitly aligns "the national cause" of Baruch the Zealot with National Socialism, more commonly known as Nazism. As she explains in her notes to the fifth radio play, "Baruch sees Jesus as the Nazi party may have seen Hitler—the Heaven-sent spell-binder, rather mad but a valuable political tool in the right hands."[13] By having Baruch make most of his political comments to Judas, who elevates his religious certitude above the words of Jesus, she implies that political certitude mirrors religious certitude. Indeed, many non-Christians turn politics into their new religion, preaching the truth of their party with more fervor than spit-spewing evangelists at a tent meeting. As Sayers explains to an Eton educator, "if boys and girls grow up imagining that Christianity has no dogma to give them, they'll give themselves over to political dogma or economic dogma in its crudest and most intransigent form."[14] This is true for people at both ends of the political spectrum. Indeed, Sayers does not let conservatives off the hook.

Murdering Truth: The Conniving Caiaphas

One of Sayers's most subtle moves in *The Man Born to Be King* didn't occur to me until I started composing this chapter. As I began writing about the political tensions between Pharisees and Zealots in Sayers's broadcasts, I suddenly realized that I had done the very thing that perpetuates polarized rhetoric; I had allowed my thoughts to fall into the grooves of cliché. Getting ready to expose the Zealot radicals as naïve in their revolutionary rhetoric, I had conceptualized Pharisees as the true villains: the ones most fully responsible for the murder of God. After all, I had been hearing about Pharisees my whole life, usually in sermons about the need to avoid Pharisaical legalism. Pharisees were denounced by Jesus more than any other group of people due to their passion for maintaining traditional practices—and judging others who didn't share their beliefs.

Sayers includes confrontations between Jesus and legalists in her radio plays. But rather than making Pharisees the villains of the story, she emphasizes the Sanhedrim (using the Hebrew spelling rather than the Aramaic *Sanhedrin*), perhaps because the Sanhedrim, composed of chief priests, elders, and scribes, had judiciary power and hence political clout. True to the Gospels, Sayers has Jesus tried before the Sanhedrim, with High Priest Caiaphas presiding over the trial. Hence, to counterbalance Baruch as political leader of a *secular* nationalist party, Sayers develops the character of High Priest Caiaphas, describing him in her character notes as "the complete *ecclesiastical* politician—a plausible and nasty piece of work."[15]

Sayers's Caiaphas is both nasty and plausible because his political concerns outweigh his religious concerns. Like many politicians then and now, he uses religious rhetoric only when it serves his best interests. Whereas the Pharisees tend to believe (if not practice) what they preach, whether for good or for ill, Caiaphas says whatever he thinks will elevate his personal glory and maintain his political power. As outlined in her notes to the sixth radio play, Sayers created him to be "a smooth and supple politician, and completely unscrupulous." Unlike wise politicians who recruit and encourage collaboration among conscientious, well-informed staff members, Caiaphas rids himself of anyone who doesn't kowtow to his desires. As Sayers puts it in her notes, "One feels that he keeps a sinister little dossier, in which the names of disaffected or rash persons are carefully noted down for future reference." Ironically, "His one moment of sincerity is when he pays homage to the politician's household god of 'expediency'" in order to get rid of Jesus.[16] This last statement provides a clue as to why Sayers characterized Caiaphas the way she did.

Sayers's "expediency" echoes the Bible verse that made Caiaphas famous. As reported in the Gospel of John, when members of the Sanhedrim gathered together to decide what to do with this nonconformist fellow named Jesus, "One of them, Caiaphas, who was high priest that year, said to them, 'You know nothing at all; you do not understand that it is expedient for you that one man should die for the people'" (John 11:49–50, RSV). Echoing the tactics of despicable politicians, Caiaphas puts down people who question him: "you know nothing at all." Furthermore, John's gospel establishes that Caiaphas interwove religious and nationalist rhetoric to justify political expediency: "he prophesied that Jesus should die for the nation, and not for the nation only, but to gather into one the children of God who are scattered abroad" (John 11:51–52, RSV). Caiaphas, in other words, preaches what we hear in political campaigns and presidencies today: people must be sacrificed in order to draw the majority together for the good of the nation. The problem, of course, is in his narrow definition of "the children of God." For Caiaphas, "children" did not include the Son of God, who celebrated outsiders like Samaritans and who embraced people who had strayed from traditional religious practices. As far as the expedient Caiaphas was concerned, children of God were those who supported a traditional nationalist cause—love it or leave it.

Sayers has Caiaphas make his famous statement twice, thus emphasizing its importance in two ways. First, of course, she wanted listeners to pick up on the irony: when Caiaphas argued it was expedient for one man to die for the people, he had no idea that his words would someday have spiritual rather than political meaning. Jesus, the Incarnate Son of God, indeed died for the people—not to save them from liberals or conservatives, but to save them from their own sinful defiance of God. This may explain why Sayers has Caiaphas make his first statement in response to Sanhedrim member Nicodemus, famous for eliciting from Jesus that subversive metaphor about "being born from above" (John 3:3). In play six, then, Sayers has Nicodemus question whether Jesus, "an innocent man," should be "liquidated," causing Caiaphas to respond, "it is sometimes expedient that one man should die for the people."[17]

But Sayers also wanted her BBC listeners to think about Caiaphas's commitment to expediency for the sake of nationalism. Hence, in the next play, she has Joseph of Arimathaea (the man who provided the tomb for Jesus) address the Sanhedrim about getting rid of Jesus, saying, "I am only anxious that an innocent person shall not be victimised." Caiaphas, the consummate politician, responds, "I said before, and I say again, that it is better to sacrifice one man, rather than the whole nation. That is not persecution; it is policy."[18] In the midst of World War II, Caiaphas's famous appeal to "expediency" took on special meaning. Wanting to make Germany great again, Hitler convinced his minions to sacrifice the Jewish "few" so that the Aryan many might prosper. As far as the Nazis were concerned, "it is not persecution; it is policy."

Sayers makes the connection between Caiaphas and Nazis explicit. In her introduction to the collected plays, she establishes that "Caiaphas was the ecclesiastical politician, appointed, like one of Hitler's bishops, by a heathen government, expressly that he might collaborate with the New Order and see that the Church toed the line drawn by the State."[19] How many times have we seen something similar in our own era: politicians appointing Christians to their campaign committees and/or cabinets to make sure evangelicals support their leadership?

Political Campaigns: Crowd Sourcing

Manipulative politicians like Baruch, Caiaphas, and Hitler, of course, would have no power without crowds of true believers passionately endorsing their campaigns. Sayers therefore uses the famous Barabbas incident (Matthew 27; Mark 15; Luke 23; John 18) to show how, in the name of nationalism, people get whipped up to support questionable, if not evil, causes. As she explains in her notes to the tenth broadcast, appropriately titled *The Princes of This World*, the Crowd (a word she capitalizes) "is so important in this play that it must be quite clear in its collective mind what it is doing. The antagonism of the people to a person so popular as Jesus seems quite inexplicable and unconvincing till we really grasp what the situation is." To intensify the situation, Sayers has a "cheer-leader" (her term) manipulate the Crowd, getting it to demand fulfillment of a tradition: "the release of the Passover prisoner." Appealing "to nationalist feeling," a phrase Sayers uses twice in one paragraph, the cheerleader gets the Crowd chanting in unison for the release of Barabbas, a known criminal, rather than for Jesus. Reminding us of political rallies in our own day when a candidate gets followers to chant slurs against opponents, the Crowd in front of Pilate's palace "becomes the strategic pivot of the campaign" against Jesus.[20] In the name of both nationalism and tradition, truth is murdered.

Sayers makes clear, however, that such tactics do not characterize one party more than another. She criticizes, instead, what she later calls "the 'nothing-but' system of interpretation which sits heavily down on one little bit"—whether sitting down on the right or the left. In contrast, the "whole truth" for Christians, she argues, is about "walking a razor-edge of delicate balance between the lop-sided exaggerations."[21] By aligning both Zealot radicals and Sanhedrim conservatives with the Nazis, Sayers forces us to question the relationship between politics and faith. Wanting Christians to assess political issues with compassionate intelligence rather than respond with Judas-like certitude, she took a stand against political manipulations like those of Baruch and Caiaphas, both of whom wanted to *use* Jesus, the Word of God, rather than to follow him.

Enslaving Jesus

Using the Word of God to support political causes has long marred Christianity. One obvious example is the way nineteenth century Americans employed the Bible to argue in support of slavery. Though many people think that such arguments were primarily made by Southerners, Christian historian Mark Noll has proven that, before the Civil War, Christians in both the North and the South "*who took most seriously* the authority of Scripture" believed that "the Bible sanctioned slavery." Quoting passages about servants obeying their masters, like Ephesians 6:5–9, believers across the country regarded the abolition of slavery as an "unbiblical" capitulation to changes in culture. In total disregard for Paul's assertion that "There is no longer Jew or Greek, there is no longer slave or free, there is no longer male and female; for all of you are one in Christ Jesus" (Galatians 3:28), antebellum Christians denounced supporters of the abolitionist cause, calling them intellectual "elites"—a slur still used today to dismiss anyone who questions a conservative agenda.[22]

Today one would be hard-pressed to find a Christian who uses Jesus or the Bible to endorse human trafficking. In fact, we celebrate those Christian abolitionists who defied tradition in order to subvert slavery. But the political controversy before and during the Civil War should force us to consider how Christians, even in our lifetimes, have used the Word of God to support certain traditional beliefs while ignoring the subversive nature of Christ's teaching. I know someone who, in the early 1980s, became pastor of a church in the South that he found to be loving and supportive—until it came to issues of race. When he talked to his congregation about the importance of integration, church members told him that the Bible endorsed segregation, and they quoted the verse "God separated the light from the darkness" (Genesis 1:4). Having grown up in the North, he was horrified that people manipulated Scripture to preserve the racist status quo. However, as with abolition, the North has been no less guilty.

In 2018, the editors of *Christianity Today* confessed that their flagship evangelical journal (founded in Abraham Lincoln's home state of Illinois) published articles in the 1950s that supported racial segregation. As editor-in-chief Mark Galli explained in 2018, "*CT* did not lead as much as reflect the moral ambiguity and confusion of that era's white evangelical churches. Though today we champion racial justice as a vital component of Christian discipleship, we must acknowledge and repent of this part of our history."[23] Fulfilling the biblical injunction to confess our sins, Galli's admission should encourage us to ponder what issues Christians promote today that reflect love of the status quo more than trust in Jesus Christ.

Significantly, during the same era that American evangelicals were endorsing segregation, Sayers wrote an essay arguing that a man invites Satan to enter through the "doors of his mind" any time "he allows the lust of division and destruction to take hold of his will; for evil thrives upon division." Identifying as despicable sin the "fear and disgust" many people have toward "difference," she asserts that different colors of skin display "a variety in the human race that ought to be pleasing and interesting." She proceeds to apply that variety to different ethnicities as well: "the minute we begin to despise and dislike another man, who has offered us no injury, simply and solely because he is 'foreign'—if we start off with a prejudice against him because he is a Jew or a Turk or a South Sea Islander . . .—then we are letting difference become division," which, she makes clear, is the utmost evil.[24]

Pagan Politics

Unfortunately, many politicians seem to encourage "the lust of division," sometimes lacing their rhetoric with religious language, as though to say only their party embodies Christian values. Rather than proclaiming "for to me, to live is Christ" (Philippians 1:21), their supporters seem to proclaim, "for me to live is my party's political agenda," turning Jesus into a luminous halo hovering over their party's platform. Sayers, in contrast, argued that "Christianity shouldn't make the mistake of identifying itself with any political or economic panacea. That is fatal—and incidentally, a thing that Christ was far too shrewd to do." It is fatal, she explains, because panacea-like solutions are "liable to be discredited by hard facts," thus making Christians seem either incredibly naïve or manipulatively self-serving.[25]

Sayers makes much the same point in an article she wrote while in the midst of composing *The Man Born to Be King*. Calling it "The Church in the New Age," she argues that the church should not become identified with any political "scheme of perfection, for in so doing she identifies herself not only with its virtues but also with its inherent errors and corruptions." Like the people who construct them, political schemes are flawed, often falling like the platform on which people hoisted William of Sens to the apex of a cathedral arch. Those witnessing the "catastrophe" will disregard, if not denounce, any church still "clinging to the rotten platform on which she has come to rely."[26]

As far as Sayers is concerned, Christians who cling to political platforms as the foundation for a better world end up echoing "pagan" religious assumptions. One kind of pagan believes that "the Golden Age lies in the past, and that man needs only make an effort to return to it." Another kind projects the ideal existence into the future, believing that humans need "only to evolve and educate" themselves in order to attain it. To drive the point home, Sayers proceeds to fancifully describe political true believers facing opposite directions, one toward the right, one toward the left, each with a pot of fruity jam "slung before his nose, in the wistful hope that if he goes fast enough he may succeed in overtaking tomorrow or catching up with yesterday," until he can eventually "sit down and eat his jam forever." Though looking in opposite directions, political pagans mirror each other, both assuming their party, and only their party, can lead the nation into a promised land, "a land flowing with milk and honey" (Exodus 33:3), if not with potted jam. Sayers, in contrast, argues that the promised land for Christians is the kingdom of God, which "is a state of the soul, and not an event in time."[27]

How, then, might Sayers help Christians today respond to the different fruity jams motivating our current (currant?) political discourse—without having us renounce jam altogether? In other words, how might Christians take the kingdom of God seriously while at the same time avoiding political quietism?

The Not-So-Quiet Sayers

The word *quietism* has both religious and political meanings. It can describe a mystical form of Christianity that emphasizes union with the divine through contemplation and suppression of one's will; or it can refer to a retreat from participation in things of the world, including any attempt to engage with humanitarian causes, whether religious or political. What both definitions have in common is passivity. *Quietism*, in other words, has never been used in a sentence about Sayers—until now, used only in order to say that she was rarely passive or ever quiet about religious and political issues she considered important.

Expressing her opinions both strongly and frequently, Sayers took time from her busy schedule to write to Members of Parliament (MPs) as well as letters to editors of popular periodicals, both religious and secular. She went to the effort of "chairing an Eve-of-the Poll meeting," which included a candidate for office. Though often "voting Conservative," especially later in life, she never once identified her political position as the *Christian* position.[28] In fact, when a member of the London Missionary Society reproached her for critiquing the Labour Party in 1950, Sayers wrote, "If you people would bother less about 'religious thought' and pay a trifle more attention to the necessity for common honesty in public matters, it would be a good thing for the Church and for the nation."[29] Rather than politicize Christianity, Sayers would have us educate ourselves in order to make intelligent choices at our polling places: choices based on research about individual candidates and issues, research that includes thoughtful conversations with people from the opposing party.

Sayers held up as an example her dear friend Helen Simpson, who ran for Parliament under the Liberal ticket. When Helen died prematurely from cancer, Sayers described her as having "one of the finest minds I know," saying in a letter to a mutual friend, "I don't think I ever met anybody who was so intensely interested in every kind of person and thing she encountered on her passage through life, and I feel that her death at this moment is a blow not only to her friends but also to the country."[30]

In a eulogy she wrote for a non-partisan journal, Sayers celebrated Helen Simpson's politics, telling us, in the process, a little bit about her own at the time: "If [Helen] had lived to take an active part in politics, she would have turned her effects most particularly to secure improved housing, a more intelligent use of medical facilities, and, above all, a better kind of education for the people of this country. . . . Her aim was directed to an education which should liberate [the British] to think with discrimination and act independently."[31] Helen, in other words, had the intelligence to think critically and the fortitude to act independently: a politician committed to the integrity of her work.

The Integrity of Work

Sayers's commitment to the integrity of work, as we have seen, helped revitalize her Christianity. In *The Zeal of Thy House*, she has her most noble characters respect the flawed architect, William of

Sens, because "He thinks of nothing, lives for nothing, but the integrity of his work."[32] It was people who ignored the integrity of work, in fact, that caused crippling catastrophe by raising William on a poorly supported platform. Several years after writing *The Zeal of Thy House*, Sayers condensed her thoughts about work into that most subversive of comments, "The only Christian work is good work well done." Though Christians on different sides of the aisle may disagree about accurate definitions of "good work," we can all benefit from Sayers's next statement, which is a quotation of Jacques Maritain: "If you want to produce Christian work, be a Christian, and try to make a work of beauty into which you have put your heart; do not adopt a Christian pose."[33] Maritain's words can speak to any nation where political true believers "adopt a Christian pose," sometimes arguing outright that anyone who fails to support their party cannot be authentically Christian.

After one of my lectures on Sayers early in 2020, a retired man told me that someone explicitly questioned his commitment to Christ because he didn't support the "correct" political party. Significantly, I had said nothing about politics in my lecture; I had primarily discussed how *The Man Born to Be King* broadcasts, reviled by Christian protectors of the status quo, led thousands to renewed faith, and I ended with Sayers's words, "The only Christian work is good work well done." The man himself applied Sayers's subversive Christianity to the political realm, intuiting what she states outright: that Jesus cannot be reduced to a conservative or liberal agenda. Whereas Sayers's Baruch dismissed Jesus as too conservative due to his refusal to lead a revolution against an unjust political system, her Caiaphas considered Jesus too liberal due to his challenge to longstanding beliefs, such as keeping the Sabbath holy. Both men, by regarding Christ through the lens of their political affiliations, contributed to the murder of God. I never mentioned Baruch or Caiaphas in my lecture; instead, this man brilliantly caught the essence of Sayers's subversive commitment to the integrity of work, even in the realm of politics.

Unfortunately, as Sayers despairs in *The Mind of the Maker*, "the integrity of the work . . . rarely figures in any scheme for an ordered society, whether issued by Labor [sic] or by Capital," i.e., the political left or the political right.[34] How, then, might Christians embedded in highly politicized environments today respond to Sayers's concern without endorsing, on the one hand, what she calls "the new religion called politics,"[35] or retreating to quietism on the other? Sayers, I believe, would have us follow principles discussed so far in this book, principles that guided her affirmation and celebration of Christian orthodoxy:

1. rather than an economy of exchange, emphasize God's gift;
2. rather than punishment, preach the judgment of consequences;
3. rather than either/or rhetoric, commit to both/and truth;
4. rather than clichés, use creative language;
5. rather than the status quo, encourage the handing over of truth;
6. rather than certitude, offer the gift of love.

Political Exchangism

As discussed in chapter 2, many Christians end up copying other religions by reducing the truth of the Gospel to an economy of exchange: do this, say this, believe this and you get the promised land in exchange. Unfortunately, when such Christians get passionate about politics, they often intensify their exchangism, duplicating what Sayers calls "pagan" practices. Talking about their own candidates as offering salvation from the evils of the opposing party, they become positively religious about the need to exchange one politician for another: *if* we put this person in power, *then* our problems will be solved. As in detective fiction, it's a matter of finding the correct solution.

In a chapter titled "Problem Picture" in *The Mind of the Maker*, Sayers critiques the way people treat governmental problems like the mysteries of detective fiction. She parallels the finishing of a detective novel with "building a wall"; once the end is achieved, "the struggle is over and finished with," at which time "we may sit back in our chairs and cease thinking." However, as she explains in the next paragraph, something like the "problem of peace and security" cannot be solved with a "magic formula" like building a wall. Magic, as we have seen, endorses an economy of exchange: say the magic word, rub the magic lamp, institute the magic program and you get your wishes in exchange. Instead of a magic formula, Sayers argues that national "peace and security" should be seen as a "work to be made"—made not by those who "adopt a Christian pose," but by those who value good work well done. And she applies this principle to people on the left as well as the right: "The man who uses violent invective against those who seek to 'uphold the *status quo*' or cling to an 'outworn tradition,' is justified in doing so *only* if he himself contemplates no fixed point of achievement ahead."[36] In other words, a magical solution, like voting the "correct" person into office as one's fixed point of achievement, is not enough. "Peace and security" depend upon "the integrity of the work" done not only by our elected officials but also by those who vote them into power.

Five and a half months after Sayers published her indictment of magic formulas for "peace and security," the BBC began broadcasting *The Man Born to Be King*, which, in addition to contrasting Baruch and Caiaphas, exposes the vexed relationship between religious and political exchangism. Sayers begins her second play, *The King's Herald*, with people chatting while on their way to see John the Baptist. A driver hired to transport a family to the baptism site is cynical about John, suggesting the Baptist represents a religious economy of exchange when what working-class people need is economic justice: "Be good and you will be happy and the Lord will provide and all the rest of it. Let Him provide decent wages, that's what I say, and I'll be happy enough." When someone retorts that John the Baptist proclaims that "the Messiah is coming to free Israel," the driver responds, "That's politics."[37] As though referring to the hope for a political savior that drives national elections, he follows up with, "steer clear of politics." Sure enough, as crowds flock to John the Baptist, someone accuses the Baptist of being politically subversive, yelling out, "I wonder the government doesn't stop this kind of thing—seditious, I call it."[38] For many people, any challenge to their beliefs, whether religious or political, reeks of treason.

Significantly, not long after the reference to "seditious" activity in Sayers's play about Christ's baptism, Judas speaks for the first time. Originally a devoted disciple of the Baptist, Judas says of John, "His mission will change the face of the world." Soon afterwards, Baruch the Zealot approaches Judas, saying, "I belong to the party that wants a free Israel."[39] Sayers thus shows religion getting mixed up with politics right from the start of Christ's ministry, implying that both attract people committed to exchange. After meeting Jesus, of course, Judas exchanges his certitude about John the Baptist for certitude about Jesus, until he eventually becomes manipulated by the politicized rhetoric of Baruch. Despite all these political manipulations, Jesus changed the face of the world not by leading a political revolution but by rising from the dead. As a wholly untraditional Messiah, God Incarnate defied religious exchangism by offering salvation as a gift.

Sayers was disturbed by the connection between religious and political exchangism even before *The Man Born to Be King* transformed the lives of thousands. As discussed in chapter 2, her 1933 detective novel *Murder Must Advertise* parallels the advertising of consumer products with the selling of cocaine. We should take note, then, when Sayers ends the entire novel by embedding religious and political statements within a list of superficial advertising slogans:

> Eat more Oats. Take Care of your Complexion. *No More War*. Shine your shoes with Shino. . . . *Prepare to meet thy God*. Bung's Beer is Better. . . . *Vote for Punkin and Protect your Profits*. Stop that Sneeze with Snuffo. Flush your Kidneys with Fizzlets. Flush your Drains with Sanfect. . . .[40]

By including in her list the religious language of "Prepare to meet thy God" along with the political language of "No More War" and "Vote for Punkin and Protect your Profits," Sayers implies that such slogans have been emptied of any significance other than as ideas people can buy (into)—like consumer products—in order to feel good about themselves. From changing one's face ("Take Care of your Complexion") to changing the face of one's world, advertising panders to economies of exchange.

Christians often buy into such advertising, believing their candidate, if exchanged for the opposition's candidate, will change the face of the world, either by returning the government to past policies or by propelling it toward promised programs. Ironically, of course, after four to eight years of a presidency, the opposite party often comes into power, many times overturning policies that the preceding party implemented with intelligence and hard work. Once again, Sayers was not arguing against Christians getting involved in state and national politics; she clearly believed we need more Helen Simpsons in the world. Instead, as a believer passionately committed to Christian orthodoxy, she considers it blasphemy to regard one party as more "Christian" than another. In her essay about the seven deadly sins, she proclaims that any effort to "make God an instrument in the service of man" is "blasphemous hypocrisy."[41] And hypocrisy more often than not has dire consequences.

The Judgment of Consequences

As discussed in chapter 2, Sayers thought a great deal about consequences, concluding that divine judgment is not *in exchange* for bad behavior, but occurs when our choices defy God's created order. In fact, one could read *The Man Born to Be King* not only as a cautionary tale about certitude, but also as a parable about consequences. The crucifixion occurs due to the consequences of sin, on both a theological and a political level: the universal consequences of humanity's fall from unity with God, as well as the particular consequences of political maneuvering. Put together, both theological and political consequences suggest that politicians' personal lives may have effects on culture far more extensive than their ability to overturn political programs established by the opposition. When Christians endorse leaders who have been caught in lies and in adultery, they perpetuate the idea that following the example of Jesus is not as important as one's political platform.

Such Christians become like members of the Sanhedrim in *The Man Born to Be King.* When one elder states, "I will say for Rome—she may be heathen, but she's certainly efficient," Sayers has Caiaphas emphatically agree, explaining that that's why they need to get rid of Jesus.[42] In other words, for many Christians, the efficiency of getting desired results—like, say, a certain kind of judge on the Supreme Court—seems more important than listening to Jesus. Rather than internalizing Christ's words about taking up the cross to follow him, repeated at least five times in the Bible, religiously driven politicos seem to follow, instead, the anti-Christian political philosopher Niccolò Machiavelli, who famously said that "the ends justify the means." The ends that concerned Sayers, in contrast, were the long-term *consequences* of our choices.

Rather than religiously endorsing one party over the other, Sayers would have us become more concerned about the judgment of consequences: the effects that the abusive rhetoric or self-indulgent lifestyle of a political leader have on cultural values. Policies can be overturned as one party's dominance is exchanged for another. But, thanks to social media, most people today are far more aware of the lies, adultery, and name-calling of political leaders than of their policies. This awareness will probably shape their future behavior, or at least the behavior of their children, far more than voting a particular party into power.

The role of the church, Sayers asserts, "is not to support any system, but to display the eternal standards by which systems are judged. . . . Her vocation, in short, is not to sanction measures, but to sanctify mankind."[43] Sanctification, as she argued for the last two decades of her life, is made possible by the death and resurrection of a both/and Christ. The church's role, in other words, is to preach the good news of God's gift.

The Heresy of Either/Or Certitude

Heartily endorsing the both/and of Christ's nature—*both* fully God *and* fully human—Sayers considered it to be the foundation upon which all Christian belief should rest, including belief in the realm of politics. One might argue, in fact, that the polarized political rhetoric dividing many Christians today reflects a heretical preference for either/or thought. Like an economy of exchange, either/or thought is much easier to understand than the shocking truth of Christ's both/and nature.

Sayers's sense of the radical contrast between God's gift of salvation and political exchangism shaped how she responded to a Liberal MP who had complimented one of her books. Writing back that she read one of his books "with much interest," she proceeds to disagree with him about communism. However, rather than argue that capitalism is the answer to the world's ills, Sayers subversively writes, "Capitalist or Communist, I cannot believe that salvation is to be found in any system which subordinates Man to Economics." Refusing to reduce salvation to either/or categories dependent upon on economies of exchange—whether capitalist or communist exchange—she instead implies the need for a both/and Savior. She goes on to practice what she preaches by suggesting to the Liberal MP "the things on which we can happily and fruitfully agree." Modeling both/and in a political discussion, Sayers clearly articulates her disagreement even as she focuses on what they have in common. And one thing they agree upon, as she proceeds to tell him, is the need for citizens "to learn to think" on their own in order to avoid being manipulated by "the next Hitler," by which she means any politician who reduces national issues to good guys versus bad guys, viciously denouncing anyone who disagrees with him.[44]

This does not mean Sayers was wishy-washy, finding commonalities with opponents in order to be nice. Few who knew Sayers would suggest that one of her weaknesses was being too nice. Instead, she worked to carefully consider as well as articulate how she both disagreed and agreed with political opponents, clearly distinguishing such both/and practices from wobbling between either/or possibilities. For example, soon after World War II ended in Europe, Sayers wrote her twenty-one-year-old son, saying "I am not now sure which will be the more dangerous—a large Socialist majority, taking its cue from Russia and offending America, or a wibbly-wobbly government of either party, with no clear majority, and wangled by the Liberal and Independent minorities."[45] Rather than manifesting the certitude of Judas, Baruch, or Caiaphas, Sayers thinks about the consequences of various political options. And her concern about a wibbly-wobbly government, whether left-leaning or right-leaning, reflects her passion about the integrity of work: good governments are led by persons so committed to doing their jobs with integrity that they do not wibble-wobble to get more votes.

Sayers so disliked wibbly-wobbly politicians that, the same year she wrote her son, she contacted an independent MP to tell him "I dislike your politics, both . . . the hedge on which you were sitting and the side on which you appear to have come down."[46] Most hedges become wibbly-wobbly when sat upon, and the recipient of Sayers's letter fell off his hedge onto the side that won the 1945 election: the Labour Party. Two years later, Sayers wrote an article for the Conservative and Unionist Central Office (the official name of the Tory Party) upholding the party's denunciation of high taxes.[47] Nevertheless, in the very same year, she published several essays that seem to question a conservative agenda.

In a book first published in 1947, *Creed or Chaos and Other Essays in Popular Theology*, Sayers reproduces several essays and lectures written during World War II. In the title piece, "Creed or Chaos?," Sayers denounces "the great economic fallacy which allows wheat and coffee to be burnt and fish to be used for manure while whole populations stand in need of food." And in "The Other Six Deadly Sins," she aligns attitudes that drive capitalism with the deadly sin of Covetousness, whose "war cries are 'Business Efficiency!' 'Free Competition!' 'Get Out or Get Under' and 'There's Always Room at the Top!'"[48] Rather than being wibbly-wobbly to curry favor, saying what she thinks listeners want to hear, Sayers passionately argues her positions, sometimes sounding like a liberal, sometimes like a conservative. Considering each issue and policy on its own merits rather than on which party endorses it, Sayers believed politics should be based on critical thinking and love for humanity rather than "the doctrinaire passion for oversimplification which refuses to take account of the complexity of human nature."[49]

Political Pride versus Christian Love

Unfortunately, rather than taking account of the complexity of human nature, many voters seem to ground their political certitude in either/or assumptions. Sayers implies as much in *The*

Emperor Constantine, her 1951 play about the either/or nature of the Arian heresy. As discussed in chapter 1, however, Sayers implies that what makes Arius *most* despicable is not his one-sided, Bible-based argument but his arrogance.[50] Considering anyone who disagrees with him either stupid or unbiblical, Arius parallels politicians in our own day who manifest what Sayers repeatedly establishes as the worst sin of all: arrogant pride.

Sayers's concern about pride, of course, is nothing new. Medieval morality plays repeatedly dramatized the personified character of Pride as the tyrannical leader whom all the other sins obey. As Sayers explains in her essay on the seven deadly sins, "the head and origin of all sin is the basic sin of *Superbia* or Pride." And she relates Pride to both religion and politics by quoting from a famous poem: "Whenever we say, whether in the personal, political, or social sphere, 'I am the master of my fate, / I am the captain of my soul,' we are committing the sin of Pride."[51]

Committed instead to Christ, whose both/and nature was established at Nicaea in defiance of Arius, Sayers repeatedly addresses the importance of humility in light of both/and thought. In her 1946 play *The Just Vengeance,* she establishes that all individuals are simultaneously innocent and guilty; all of us have acted like *both* Abel *and* Cain. As a character in *Just Vengeance* puts it, "Do not you all / Suffer with Abel and destroy with Cain, / Each one at once the victim and the avenger?"[52] She illustrates this principle with the politics of World War II. Her protagonist, an airman during the war, agonizes over the fact that bombs England dropped on Germany killed thousands of people, "the guiltless along with the guilty." Nevertheless, failure to drop those bombs would send thousands of others to suffering and "death in a concentration camp." When it comes to the politics of war, both justice and injustice are equally "cruel," as Sayers puts it, summarizing the problem as "the injustice of justice."[53] It is the both/and of sin, redeemed only by a both/and Savior.

Believing her both/and Savior to be just as relevant during peacetime, Sayers repeatedly subverted either/or categories in politics. In her essay about "The Church in the New Age" she argues that the church "must call for a more equitable distribution of wealth": a goal most people would identify with liberalism, if not socialism. But then she immediately goes on to say that the church "must not back Communism or Socialism against Capitalism, for she may not admit the *false assumption behind all three*—that man lives by bread alone, and that the basis of society is economic."[54] Affirming Christ's repeated teaching about caring for the needs of others, both physical and spiritual, Sayers suggests that Christians, whether from the right or from the left, drown out the voice of Jesus when they turn economic policies into their bread of salvation.

Inspired by her belief in Christ as the bread of salvation, Sayers sent literal food to someone whose home was bombed during the war, reinforcing that Christianity is *both* belief in a gift *and* relief offered through our own gifts. Making her both/and behavior downright shocking is the fact that she sent the gifs to a self-proclaimed Nazi: her childhood piano teacher who, upon returning to Germany, embraced Hitler's vision for Aryan supremacy. Nevertheless, despite her abhorrence of Nazi certitude, Sayers put the needs of a person above politics, explaining her motivation in a 1944 poem so powerful that it was published in America's *Atlantic Monthly* as well as in England's *Fortnightly*. Explicitly acknowledging the Fräulein's support of the Fuehrer in her poem, Sayers ends by saying "The solidarity of mankind is a solidarity in guilt, / and all our virtues stand in need of forgiveness."[55] Sayers refuses either/or categories, asserting a both/and truth: we are all *both* Cain *and* Abel, *both* victims *and* victimizers, our "solidarity in guilt" surmounted by the gift of forgiveness God offers to the entire world (John 3:16).

Incarnational versus Gnostic Politics

Ironically, all too many Christians think that they reveal the strength of their faith by establishing unwavering solidarity only with people who passionately agree with them. They thus mirror those who, scornful of Christianity, consider a both/and approach to politics as outrageously impossible as the both/and of Christ's nature. For Sayers, in contrast, anyone who endorses the both/and of the incarnation should want to model, in all areas of life, the significance of God taking on human flesh.

One of the basic principles of flesh is that it is shaped by the time and location where it takes life. This explains Sayers's vision behind *The Man Born to Be King*: "Jesus Christ is unique—unique among gods and men. There have been incarnate gods a-plenty, and slain-and-resurrected gods not a few; but He is the only God who has a date in history."[56] Born into history, Jesus reflected his culture even as he challenged it: his parables are about sheep and Samaritans, oil lamps and vineyards. No Bible reader today would protest that Jesus seems out of touch with reality because he fails to talk about mass transit and flush toilets.

Nevertheless, when it comes to politics, those same people often discount the incarnated experience of their opponents, saying things like "He votes that way only because he's a millionaire," or "She votes that way because she is a single mother." Well of course! The location of their bodies influences their perceptions of reality! This profound incarnational truth explains Sayers's ability to have compassion even for a Nazi. As she makes clear repeatedly in her writings, all humans, being flesh, see in a mirror darkly: a mirror that reflects both the Cain of our fleshly interests as well as our Abel-like desire for truth. To deny this is to commit another either/or heresy that Sayers repeatedly mentions in her correspondence: Gnosticism.

As David Lyle Jeffrey and Martin E. Marty explain in their overview of Christian heresies, "Gnostics had two central preoccupations: belief in a dualistic world in which good and evil contested; and belief in the existence of a secret code of true knowledge passed on from one master 'knower' to the next."[57] The relevance to the political environment in Sayers's day, as well as our own, is obvious. True believers from both the right and the left act as though their party has attained disembodied "true knowledge" about what's best for the country, and that's why they're passionate about fighting a dualistic battle of good versus evil, their party, of course, taking the side of the angels. Warped by political Gnosticism—what Sayers calls "Knowledge with a capital K"[58]—they fail to consider how the experience of their own bodies affects their knowledge, thus ignoring how they, like their opponents, are both Cain and Abel.

How, then, do we respond to politicized either/or heresies while endorsing the incarnation of truth? Sayers would answer with the mind of the maker.

The Political Mind of the Maker

It is easy to forget that Sayers originally conceptualized *The Mind of the Maker* (1941) as a political document. Not long after the start of World War II, she and two of her closest friends offered their services as writers for Britain's Ministry of Information, with the goal of "disseminating encouraging ideas." They quickly discovered, however, that the government agency was, in Sayers's inimitable words, an "overcrowded monkey-house of graft and incompetence."[59] The three therefore decided to initiate their own project of encouragement. Calling it *Bridgeheads*, they invited writers they knew to compose works that might influence common citizens to respond with creativity rather than despair while facing the horrors of war. Significantly, one of the two friends brainstorming the enterprise with Sayers was the politically liberal Helen Simpson.

We know about the goals of *Bridgeheads* from a proposal that most scholars believe was written by Sayers. Called "Statement of Aims for the proposed *Bridgehead* series of books," it confirms many things discussed in this chapter so far:

- an emphasis that "nationalism must not be 'deified'"
- the importance of critical thinking, to the point of "demand[ing]" that the British government spend "necessary money for . . . better education"
- the refusal to reduce politics to the either/or of "dialectical opposites"
- a both/and "balance between the individual and the community"
- "the importance of the creative arts," as well as securing for the arts "national and political recognition."[60]

Sayers had all these things in mind when she wrote *The Mind of the Maker*, which was the first book published in the *Bridgehead* series.

In her book, as discussed in the preceding chapter, Sayers suggests that creativity is trinitarian: a new Idea is inseparable from its incarnated Energy, and both together generate Power. The mind of the maker leads to embodied acts of creativity through works that can affect others, whether painted, printed, pronounced, or performed. Even common everyday language can reflect incarnated thought. People often remember the person that creatively shocked them into new perceptions: the teacher imaginatively presenting subversive insight; the pastor making the Gospel come alive; the friend using a provocative metaphor. As Sayers puts it, "It is of the nature of the word to reveal itself and to incarnate itself—to take material form."[61]

In contrast, clichés are disembodied terms or phrases that people unthinkingly repeat, usually because they reinforce a Gnostic "code of true knowledge." Terms like *fake news* or *political correctness*, for example, have been used by people to discount anything that challenges their political "knowledge," thus emptying the words *fake* and *correctness* of any significant meaning. Rather than fulfilling the *imago Dei*, such cliché-mongers spew, like gargoyles at the end of water gutters, meaningless rhetoric: "Words which should be living fall from their lips like stones, lacking the spirit of wisdom, which is the life."[62] Indeed, once you hear one cliché from a political true believer, whether from the right or the left, you often can predict every other opinion he or she holds. That's not creativity; it's conformism; that's not the image of the Trinity, it's the trite. Either way, as Sayers put it in a book that immediately preceded *The Mind of the Maker*, "many people contrive never once to think for themselves from the cradle to the grave."[63]

Sayers encourages Christians to stand apart by thinking for themselves, fulfilling the *imago Dei* through their creativity.

Convinced that artists can affect politics, she encourages "creative citizenship," arguing that the *imago Dei* can shock politicians out of their complacency: "At the irruption of the artist into a State department, officialdom stands aghast, not relishing the ruthless realism which goes directly to essentials." By exposing the clichés shaping contemporary thought, by illuminating how technology destabilizes human psychology, by creating sympathy for marginalized people, by depicting how unbridled capitalism warps the greedy as well as those they manipulate, "artists are dangerous people and a *subversive* element in the state."[64]

Sayers herself exemplified "the irruption of the artist into a State department" when controversy over her radio plays about Jesus landed on the floor of Parliament. Nearly a century earlier another Christian writer across the Atlantic proved to be "a subversive element in the state." In *Uncle Tom's Cabin* (1851), Harriet Beecher Stowe "provided one of the era's most powerful examples of the abolitionist appeal to the general spirit of the Bible," making many protectors of convention angry.[65] Decades later, of course, promoters of change criticized Stowe's Uncle Tom for his excessively submissive attitude toward those with white privilege. Sayers, having herself been criticized by people from *both* the right *and* the left, might summarize Stowe's effect on culture with a statement she includes in *The Mind of Maker*: "The most one can say is that between the poet and his age there is an intimate connection of mutual influence, highly complex and various, and working in all directions of time and space."[66] Stowe, in other words, challenged the language of culture even as she was shaped by it. It's the both/and of "mutual influence." In fact, Sayers's statement about "the poet and *his* age" reflects the both/and of "mutual influence" as well. Though herself a female poet who challenged culture (most of her staged plays were in verse), she still used the gendered language her era taught as most grammatically correct. We are all both Abel and Cain, both victim and victimizer.

Nevertheless, both Stowe and Sayers radically changed the way people thought about the relationship between Christ and culture. How, then, can non-artistic, un-poetic Christians help culture?

Incarnated Creativity

As discussed in chapter 4, creativity in common speech can reflect the *imago Dei* as much as the work of great authors: "If the common man is to enjoy the divinity of his humanity, he can come to it only in virtue and right of his making."[67] It's about making a difference by making new language. Instead of using clichés that perpetuate polarized thought, it means generating language that acknowledges what is good about one's opposition as well as what is problematic about one's own party, for we are all both Cain and Abel; to deny this is a form of dishonesty. As Sayers explains to an undergraduate at Cambridge University, "One must not misrepresent matters, even in the interests of one's own dogmatic convictions."[68]

Sayers's theory about the Power of creative language is once again connected to her belief in the incarnation: like the Incarnate Christ, our flesh takes life in a certain place and time of history. That, in fact, may explain why *The Man Born to Be King* and Stowe's *Uncle Tom's Cabin* were so influential: each author reflected her era even as she challenged it, enabling readers and listeners to understand enough in order to be shocked. Both authors were committed to the "handing over" of tradition.

Sayers would encourage Christians who are not authors to follow their example, if on a smaller scale, by creating new metaphors that make sense to the time and place in which we live. Consider, for example, how the mind of the maker was incarnated by one of my pastors in the suburbs of Chicago. In a sermon on Paul's letters to the Thessalonians, Pastor Jonathan mentioned the historical polarization between those believing that Christ will return before "the Tribulation," and those who argue the second coming will occur after "the Tribulation." Rather than endorse the either/or of a "Pre-Trib" or "Post-Trib" position, John said he was "Chicago Trib." Titters from the pews died down as worshippers internalized the profundity of his point: rather than obsess over something that neither the Bible nor Ecumenical Councils make clear, Christians should focus more on the dire needs of humanity in the here and now, needs reported daily in the *Chicago Tribune*. What made the remark effective was John's creative use of humor to subvert comfortable assumptions, forcing listeners to think rather than to defensively protect one side over the other: a tactic exemplified by Sayers throughout this book.

Most of us do not have Pastor Jonathan's wry humor or Sayers's subversive wit. But we all have the ability to put phrases together in ways that might discourage people from lobbing weaponized words towards enemies that lie either to the left or the right of them. Entrenched in "the new religion called politics," such people fail to realize how their trenches have become "silted up with rumbling phrases and heavy-handed veneration."[69]

Handing Over the Tradition

Recognizing that we are all both Cain and Abel, Sayers believes that fruitful change happens better from within a community than by way of attacks from without. After all, when people feel beleaguered by enemies from the outside, they often hunker down all the more, seeking protection by burying themselves in the silt of rumbling phrases. Sayers makes her views on this issue quite clear: "I object strongly to having all sorts of accusations against the Church made by outsiders. . . . But there is surely every reason why the Church herself should accuse herself."[70] Rather than obsessively working to denounce the enemy, she encourages Christians to take a hard look at how their own rhetoric and behavior undermine the subversive message of Christ. She would say something similar about a political party: beliefs and practices must be inspected, analyzed, and challenged by those who embrace them. Rather than mindless advocacy, Sayers encourages the handing over of traditional assumptions within a community itself, as discussed in chapter 3.[71]

But she also encourages love: not simply love within a community, but love for those outside who attack it. It's both/and. Take, for example, Sayers's response to Kathleen Nott, the atheist discussed in chapter 1 who reviled Sayers and C. S. Lewis in print for being "braver and stupider" than other Christian authors.[72] Though incensed by Nott's "savage attack,"[73] as she calls it, Sayers was open to conversation with her apparent enemy: "If Miss Nott were here now, she and I could establish the Kingdom of Heaven between ourselves immediately—that is, we could *if* we could. It is quite simple: she has only to love me as well as she loves herself, and I have only to love her as well as I love myself, and there is the Kingdom." Sayers goes on to admit, however, that such selfless love is easier said than done: "worm-eaten with original sin, I acknowledge that I might find it difficult." Asserting that Christlike "charity is precisely a readiness to love the unlovable," Sayers makes clear in her response to Nott that "love and charity" do not operate according to an economy of exchange: "You cannot buy them in the market and slap them on to a situation like plasters [Band-Aids]."[74]

Rather than responding to Nott with desires for justice, or even for vengeance, Sayers modeled an attitude toward her detractor consonant with what she wrote in *The Just Vengeance*. In that play, she has the citizens of Lichfield perform a rendition of the Gospel story for the recently killed airman. In the play within the play, the actor playing Jesus tells Pilate, "there is no justice in the Gospel, / There's only love."[75] God subverts an economy of exchange implied by those who demand "justice" by offering salvation as a gift made possible by the loving work of a both/and Christ. It is this play, in fact, where Sayers suggests that we are all *both* Abel *and* Cain, perhaps with a pun on the name *Abel*. Though *able* to love God and our enemies, it is easier to choose the resentment of Cain, who was motivated by an economy of exchange. Indeed, when Cain didn't win favor from God, he murdered the one who did. Nevertheless, God offered Cain an unmerited gift of salvation: the so-called "Mark of Cain" that protected him from slaughter.[76]

Giving Birth to Future Gifts

Grateful for God's unmerited gift of salvation, Sayers exercised her own gifts in creative support of a London mission. This mission, however, did not "harry prostitutes or swoop on night-clubs," as she explains to a church vicar.[77] Named after the mother of the Virgin Mary, the Society of St. Anne instead encouraged interaction between skeptics and believers, hosting debates while also providing instruction and discussion on contemporary cultural trends and issues. Knowing that "ideas can't be violently imposed on people,"[78] Sayers encouraged education and conversation that might help those on both the right and the left grapple with the complexity of religious and political issues. Significantly, it was the Society of St. Anne that decided to host a conversation between Kathleen Nott and some of the Christians she attacked: C. S. Lewis, T. S. Eliot, and D. L. Sayers. After agreeing to the debate, Nott decided at the last minute not to attend because the most prestigious Christian at the time, T. S. Eliot, could not participate. Sayers showed up and delivered her comments about love nonetheless.

Providing leadership for the Society of St. Anne until the end of her life, Sayers echoed the preaching as well as the practice of the first four Ecumenical Councils, establishing that truth is embodied, truth is communitarian, truth is both/and. When it comes to the realm of politics, we are all both Cain and able.

CHAPTER SIX
A BRIEF SUBVERSIVE CONCLUSION

This conclusion is subversive because, like Sayers, it refuses to conclude.

In *The Mind of the Maker*, Sayers poses a problem with conclusions: "The desire to solve a living problem by a definitive and sterile conclusion is natural enough; it is part of the material will to death."[1] In contrast, the will to life in Christ is about ongoing change; God is not done with us yet. The full conclusion only arrives at the moment we meet our Creator face to face—if even then. God, whose very nature is to create the new, has amazing things in store for us. Until that time, Sayers would have us fulfill the *imago Dei:* created in God's image we create new things. Doing so, we play our part in "a *living* tradition whose essence persists unchanged while its expressions continually develop."[2]

Keeping Christian tradition alive, then, depends on our commitment to new expressions that uphold ancient truth, thus shocking people with the old and the new simultaneously. And the shock of the truth for Sayers always endorses the incarnation: not only the incarnation of God in Christ, but also the incarnation—the embodiment—of those who resist change, Christians and skeptics alike. For her it is a matter of loving people who do not see things the way we do, and love means empathizing rather than reviling. We mirror the mind of our Maker by the way we create meaning for those we consider blind.

Significantly, a man born blind sent a letter to Sayers ten years after *The Man Born to Be King* subversively led hundreds to see the light for the first time in their lives. Writing to thank her, the man expressed how "convincing" Sayers had made the experience of Jacob, the man born blind, in one of her radio plays. Humbled by his gratitude, Sayers wrote him back, explaining that she was able to hand over the story from John 9 because, using her imagination, she built upon experiences of a man born blind she had known in Oxford. Paying attention to a blind man's embodied experience as he entered rooms and wandered through winding streets, she was able to make meaning for someone totally different than herself.[3] Endorsing embodiment, Sayers radically affirmed that truth is incarnational.

She also affirmed that truth is both/and, like the Incarnate Christ. Believing that Christians who reduce religion or politics to polarized either/or categories echo ancient heresies of the Church, Sayers encourages us to follow the subversive example of Christ. For her this means openness to difference and empathy for those unlike us, not in spite of, but due to belief in God Incarnate. Unlike the scribes and Pharisees who rejected the man born blind once he affirmed a different expression of truth than the one they idolized, Jacob saw God with new eyes. Sayers helps us, as well, to see with new eyes, even as she encourages us to enlighten others by fulfilling the *imago Dei*.

The year before she concluded her life on earth, Sayers was part of a commission in which "two parties" in disagreement had created a "deadlock," as she puts it. By drawing attention to a foundational document, however, Sayers soon had the opposing parties "enthusiastically" agreeing with each other, which led them to request she "draw up a formal Report, embodying all the new conclusions." As with her repeated appeal to the Nicene Creed and its affirmation of an "embodying" God, Sayers was able to guide new conclusions by appealing to a foundational document. But that was not all; she enabled the commission's antagonists to build on the foundation by creating new language. Reporting the incident to her friend Barbara Reynolds, Sayers said of the two parties, "none of them know how to handle words, so that they are apt to phrase things quite offensively, without in the least realising it." For her, new words can lead to new conclusions that reinforce rather than destroy shared foundations. "Nobody," as members of the two parties told her, "could do it so well as Miss Sayers."[4]

Believing in a both/and Christ who suffered torture and death at the hands of people very much like us, Sayers despaired over so-called believers who seem more committed to defying their enemies than to communicating subversive truth: that the Creator of the universe offers reconciliation—*at-one-ment*—as a gift to the entire world. Affirming that all have been made in the image of that Creator, Sayers encourages us to communicate the gift by offering our gifts to others, exercising creativity that might draw more people to the hospitality of a house not made with hands. If a subversive new belief or a subversive new practice does not alter the solid foundation proclaimed in the Nicene Creed, she would encourage us to discuss that belief or practice with genuine openness as to whether it might buttress and even enhance the architecture of Christian faith. After all, as Sayers well knew, the Father's house, having many mansions, does not end. Instead, it builds new conclusions on an unchanging foundation, welcoming more and more people to live and move and have their being in a house continually renewed by the word of God, which has no conclusion.

NOTES

Introduction

1. C. S. Lewis, "Cross-Examination," in *God in the Dock: Essays on Theology and Ethics*, ed. Walter Hooper (Grand Rapids, MI: Eerdmans, 1970), 260. For Lewis's delight in Sayers's correspondence, see his letter to her dated December 14, 1945, in *The Collected Letters of C. S. Lewis*, vol. 2, *Books, Broadcasts, and the War, 1931–1949*, ed. Walter Hooper (San Francisco: HarperSanFrancisco, 2004), 682. Douglas Gresham reports that the first time he saw his stepfather cry was when Lewis heard of Sayers's death. (Live interview with the author, August 2018.)

2. C. S. Lewis, letter to the editor of *Encounter*, January 1963, in *The Collected Letters of C. S. Lewis*, vol. 3, *Narnia, Cambridge, and Joy, 1950–1963*, ed. Walter Hooper (San Francisco: HarperSanFrancisco, 2007), 1400.

3. According to Ross Douthat, the term "nones" was coined by Robert Putnam and David Campbell. See *Bad Religion: How We Became a Nation of Heretics* (New York: Free Press, 2012), 142.

4. Dorothy L. Sayers to Rev. T. A. O'Neil and Rev. A. M. Stack, March 21, 1940, *The Letters of Dorothy L. Sayers*, vol. 2, *1937 to 1943, From Novelist to Playwright*, ed. Barbara Reynolds (Cambridge: Dorothy L. Sayers Society, 1997), 156.

5. Sayers to Ivy Shrimpton, March 4, 1927, *The Letters of Dorothy L. Sayers*, vol 1, *1899 to 1936: The Making of a Detective Novelist*, ed. Barbara Reynolds (New York: St. Martin's, 1995), 257.

6. Sayers, "The Gargoyle," in *The Poetry of Dorothy L. Sayers*, ed. Ralph E. Hone (Cambridge: The Dorothy L. Sayers Society, 1996), 24.

7. Sayers, "The Mocking of Christ," in *Catholic Tales and Christian Songs* (Oxford: Blackwell, 1918), 45, 48.

8. "The Mocking of Christ," 46–48.

9. Sayers to her parents, June 14, 1918, *Letters*, 1:138; Sayers to her father, November 20, 1918, *Letters*, 1:142; Sayers to Muriel Jaeger, November 22, 1918, *Letters*, 1:143.

10. Sayers, "The Greatest Drama Ever Staged," in *Creed or Chaos?* (Manchester, NH: Sophia Institute, 1974), 6.

11. Sayers, "The Christ of the Creeds," in *The Christ of the Creeds and Other Broadcast Messages to the British People during World War II*, ed. Suzanne Bray (Cambridge: The Dorothy L. Sayers Society, 2008), 34.

12. Sayers, "Greatest Drama Ever Staged," 7.

13. Sayers, "The Church's Responsibility," in *The Life of the Church and the Order of Society, Being the Proceedings of the Archbishop of York's Conference: Malvern 1941* (London: Longmans, 1942), 58.

14. Sayers to George Purkis, January 27, 1949, *The Letters of Dorothy L. Sayers*, vol. 3, *1944 to 1950: A Noble Daring*, ed. Barbara Reynolds (Cambridge: Dorothy L. Sayers Society, 1998), 424.

15. Sayers to F. H. Jaegar, July 23, 1941, *Letters*, 2:281.

16. For an overview of this process, see Pauline Adams, *Somerville for Women: An Oxford College 1879–1993* (Oxford: Oxford University Press, 1996), chapter 7.

17. Queen Victoria to William Gladstone, May 6, 1870, quoted in *The Longman Anthology of British Literature: The Victorian Age*, ed. Heather Henderson and William Sharpe, 3rd ed. (New York: Person Longman, 2006), 1655.

18. Sayers to Doris Langley Moore, November 1, 1950, *Letters*, 3:522.

19. Sayers to Maurice B. Reckitt, July 12, 1941, *Letters*, 2:275.

20. Sayers, "The Human-Not-Quite-Human," in *Are Women Human?* (Grand Rapids, MI: Eerdmans, 1971), 68–69.

21. Sayers to Marjorie Barber, October 26, 1942, *Letters*, 2:380.

22. Sayers, "The Dogma Is the Drama," in *Creed or Chaos?* (Manchester, NH: Sophia Institute, 1974), 22.

23. Sayers, "Greatest Drama Ever Staged," 8.

24. Sayers, "Dogma is the Drama," 21.

25. Sayers, "Dogma is the Drama," 22.

26. Sayers, "Dogma is the Drama," 20.

27. Sayers to Mrs. Stevenson, April 6, 1938, *Letters*, 2:71.

28. Sayers to John Wren-Lewis, Good Friday, March 1954, *The Letters of Dorothy L. Sayers*, vol. 4, *1951 to 1957: In the Midst of Life*, ed. Barbara Reynolds (Cambridge: Dorothy L. Sayers Society, 2000), 139.

29. Sayers to the Bishop of Winchester, March 17, 1942, *Letters*, 2:356.

30. Sayers, "Dogma is the Drama," 24.

31. Sayers to James Welch, July 25, 1946, *Letters*, 3:249.

32. Sayers to Father Herbert Kelly, July 24, 1947, *Letters*, 3:319.

33. Sayers to L. T. Duff, May 10, 1943, *Letters*, 2:404.

34. Sayers to R. Stephen Talmage, April 12, 1954, *Letters*, 4:153.

35. Sayers to Maurice Browne, November 22, 1946, *Letters*, 3:277.

36. Sayers, Introduction to *The Man Born to Be King* (Grand Rapids, MI: Eerdmans, 1979), 21.

Chapter 1

1. Sayers to Charles Williams, September 26, 1944, *Letters*, 3:85.

2. Sayers to Rev. W. A. W. Jarvis, January 10, 1946, *Letters*, 3:193.

3. Leroy Lad Panek, *Watteau's Shepherds: The Detective Novel in Britain 1914–1940* (Bowling Green, OH: Bowling Green University Popular Press, 1979), 72.

4. John Gross, *The New Oxford Book of Literary Anecdotes* (Oxford: Oxford University Press, 2006), 267.

5. Sayers, "Gaudy Night," in *The Art of the Mystery Story: A Collection of Critical Essays*, ed. Howard Haycraft (New York: Simon & Schuster, 1946), 210.

6. Sally Munt, *Murder by the Book: Feminism and the Crime Novel* (London: Routledge, 1994), 10.

7. Sayers, *Gaudy Night* (New York: HarperCollins, 1995), 48; *The Zeal of Thy House*, in *Four Sacred Plays* (London: Gollancz, 1948), 40 (emphases mine).

8. Sayers, *Zeal of Thy House*, 46.

9. Sayers, *Zeal of Thy House*, 101.

10. Sayers to John Wren-Lewis, Good Friday, March 1954, *Letters*, 4:139.

11. Sayers, "Greatest Drama Ever Staged," 6.

12. Sayers, "Greatest Drama Ever Staged," 6, 9.

13. Sayers, "Dogma Is the Drama," 25.

14. Sayers to John Wren-Lewis, Good Friday, March 1954, *Letters*, 4:139.

15. Sayers, *Zeal of Thy House*, 66.

16. Sayers, Introduction to *Man Born to Be King*, 6, 7, 19 (emphasis hers).

17. Sayers, Introduction to *Man Born to Be King*, 7.

18. Sayers to James Welch, September 30, 1942, *Letters*, 2:375. About "abusive telephone calls," see note 1 on page 341 of the same volume.

19. Barbara Reynolds, *Letters*, 3:428, note 2.

20. Quoted in Kathryn Wehr, "The Psalms Hidden in the Slang," *Church Times* (March 24, 2017): 20.

21. J. W. Welch, Foreword to *The Man Born to Be King: A Play-Cycle on the Life of Our Lord and Saviour Jesus Christ*, by Dorothy L. Sayers (London: Gollancz, 1946), 14.

22. Sayers, *Man Born to Be King*, 105.

23. Quoted in David Coomes, *Dorothy L. Sayers: A Careless Rage for Life* (Oxford: Lion Publishing, 1992), 18.

24. Sayers, Introduction to *Man Born to Be King*, 6.

25. Sayers to Val Gielgud, December 22, 1941, *Letters*, 2:338.

26. Sayers to James Welch, January 6, 1942, *Letters*, 2:339.

27. Welch, Foreword to *Man Born to Be King*, 15.

28. See Sayers *Letters*, 3:348, 381; 4:181; Mary Brian Durkin, "Dorothy L. Sayers: A Christian Humanist for Today," *Christian Century* (November 14, 1979): 129.
29. Quoted in Welch, Foreword to *Man Born to Be King*, 14.
30. Sayers, Introduction to *Man Born to Be King*, 3.
31. Sayers to Dorothy Rowe, October 8, 1915, *Letters*, 1:114. In a footnote on page 115, editor Barbara Reynolds informs readers about the brandy.
32. Quoted in Barbara Reynolds, *The Passionate Intellect: Dorothy L. Sayers's Encounter with Dante* (Kent, OH: Kent State University Press, 1989), 97.
33. Sayers to John Anthony Fleming, March 30, 1946, *Letters*, 3:219.
34. The comment is an addendum made by editor Barbara Reynolds following a letter that Sayers sent to her son, *Letters*, 3:243.
35. Sayers, "The Meaning of Purgatory," in *Introductory Papers on Dante* (London: Methuen, 1954), 93.
36. Sayers to Irene Amesbury, June 1, 1945, *Letters*, 3:150.
37. Sayers to Roger Newsom, December 15, 1948, *Letters*, 3:413. For C. S. Lewis's commitment to doctrine established by the first four Ecumenical Councils, see Suzanne Bray, "C. S. Lewis as an Anglican," in *Persona and Paradox: Issues of Identity for C. S. Lewis, His Friends and Associates*, ed. Suzanne Bray and William Gray (Newcastle upon Tyne, GB: Cambridge Scholars Publishing, 2012), 19–36.
38. Sayers to Maynard D. Follin, July 23, 1942, *Letters*, 2:367.
39. Sayers to the Rev. Dr. James Parkes, August 25, 1944, *Letters*, 3:51.
40. Sayers, *The Emperor Constantine: A Chronicle* (Grand Rapids, MI: Eerdmans, 1976), 143; Janice Brown, *The Seven Deadly Sins* (Kent, OH: Kent State University Press, 1998), 302.
41. Sayers, "A Debate Deferred: The Dogma in the Manger," *VII: An Anglo-American Literary Review* 3 (1982): 36.
42. Sayers to G. C. Piper, January 24, 1939, *Letters*, 2:114.
43. Sayers mentions annoyance with the "personal angle" so often in her letters that editor Barbara Reynolds puts "personal angle"

as a separate index entry for both volume 3 and 4 of Sayers's correspondence.

44. Sayers to J. C. Heenan, August 31, 1940, *Letters*, 2:180.

45. Nott, Kathleen. *The Emperor's Clothes* (Bloomington, IN: Indiana University Press, 1958), 31, 68, 43, 298.

46. Sayers to the editor of *The Spectator*, July 13, 1940, in *Letters*, 2:170. Sayers was responding to a piece in *The Spectator* written by Dr. William Boothby Selbie, a portion of which appears on the preceding page of *Letters*, vol. 2.

47. Sayers to Eric Fenn, January 21, 1941, *Letters*, 2:233.

48. Sayers to Irene Amesbury, June 1, 1945, *Letters*, 3:150.

49. Sayers, Introduction to *The Man Born to Be King*, 2.

50. Sayers to the editor of *Punch*, April 6, 1938, *Letters*, 2:73.

51. Sayers, "The Sacrament of Matter," in *The Christ of the Creeds and Other Broadcast Messages to the British People during World War II*, ed. Suzanne Bray (West Sussex, GB: The Dorothy L. Sayers Society, 2008), 40 (emphasis hers).

52. Sayers to S. Dark, editor of *The Church Times*, April 6, 1938, *Letters*, 2:72.

53. Sayers, "Greatest Drama Ever Staged," 3, 6.

54. Jaroslav Pelikan, *The Christian Tradition: A History of the Development of Doctrine. Volume One: The Emergence of the Catholic Tradition (100–600)* (Chicago, IL: University of Chicago Press, 1971), 75.

55. Sayers to Ellen Blad, July 9, 1948, *Letters*, 3:386.

56. Sayers is writing Lewis about "experimenting in a new way" while translating Dante (November 18, 1949, *Letters*, 3:465). She quotes the same Latin phrase in a letter to Professor G. L. Bickersteth in order to reference the power of her translation to *move* people's thoughts. See *Letters*, 3:468. Though some scholars question whether Galileo ever pronounced his oft-quoted words, the phrase has become important to people who have been reviled for questioning the status quo—like Sayers. See Stillman Drake, *Galileo at Work: His Scientific Biography* (Mineola, NY: Dover, 2003), 357.

Chapter 2

1. Sayers, "Why Work?," in *Creed or Chaos?* (Manchester, NH: Sophia Institute, 1974), 70.
2. Laura K. Simmons, *Creed without Chaos: Exploring Theology in the Writings of Dorothy L. Sayers* (Grand Rapids, MI: Baker Academic, 2005), 46.
3. Sayers, *Murder Must Advertise* (New York: HarperCollins, 1995), 251.
4. Sayers, *Murder Must Advertise*, 188.
5. Sayers, *Murder Must Advertise*, 188.
6. Sayers, "The Other Six Deadly Sins," in *Creed or Chaos?* (Manchester, NH: Sophia Institute, 1974), 92.
7. Sayers, "Other Six Deadly Sins," 94.
8. Sayers, *The Mind of the Maker* (San Francisco: HarperCollins, 1979), 204.
9. Derrida, not coincidentally, uses the term "counterfeit money" to highlight problems with exchangism. See Jacques Derrida, *Given Time: 1. Counterfeit Money*, trans. Peggy Kamuf (Chicago, IL: University of Chicago Press, 1994).
10. Sayers to Dr. George S. Purkis, January 27, 1949, *Letters*, 3:424, 425.
11. Richard Rorty, *Consequences of Pragmatism: Essays, 1972–1980* (Minneapolis, MN: University of Minnesota Press, 1982), 166–67.
12. Richard Rorty, quoting Donald Davidson, in *Contingency, Irony and Solidarity* (Cambridge: Cambridge University Press, 1989), 50.
13. Sayers to P. A. Micklem, Provost of Derby, March 21, 1940, *Letters*, 2:158.
14. Sayers, "The Gospel is a thing of terror," in *The Christ of the Creeds and Other Broadcast Messages to the British People during World War II*, ed. Suzanne Bray (West Sussex, GB: The Dorothy L. Sayers Society, 2008), 77.
15. Sayers, "Creed or Chaos?," in *Creed or Chaos?* (Manchester, NH: Sophia Institute, 1974), 28–29.

16. Sayers, "Creed or Chaos?," 31.

17. Sayers, "The Religions Behind the Nation," in *The Church Looks Ahead: Broadcast Talks* (London: Faber, 1941), 70.

18. Sayers, "The Christ of the Creeds," in *The Christ of the Creeds and Other Broadcast Messages to the British People during World War II*, ed. Suzanne Bray (West Sussex, GB: The Dorothy L. Sayers Society, 2008), 33.

19. Sayers, "The Triumph of Easter," in *Creed or Chaos?* (Manchester, NH: Sophia Institute, 1974), 12–13.

20. Sayers, "Triumph of Easter," 15.

21. Sayers to George S. Purkis, January 27, 1949, *Letters*, 3:424.

22. Sayers to her parents, March 23, 1910, *Letters*, 1:40.

23. Sayers to Ivy Shrimpton, April 15, 1930, *Letters*, 1:306.

24. For a detailed discussion of biographical disparities, see the first chapter of my book *Writing Performances: The Stages of Dorothy L. Sayers* (New York: Palgrave, 2004). Differing interpretations of Sayers's confirmation are discussed on page 29.

25. Sayers to Father Herbert Kelly, October 4, 1937, *Letters*, 2:48.

26. John Calvin, *Institutes of the Christian Religion*, 4.14.4, 4.17.15; quoted in Dominic Manganiello, "Transubstantiation," *A Dictionary of Biblical Tradition in English Literature*, ed. David Lyle Jeffrey (Grand Rapids, MI: Eerdmans, 1992), 775.

27. David William Bebbington, *Evangelicalism in Modern Britain: A History from the 1730s to the 1980s* (London: Unwin Hyman, 1989).

28. Sayers to C. S. Lewis, August 5, 1946, *Letters*, 3:255.

29. Sayers to John Wren-Lewis, Good Friday, March 1954, *Letters*, 4:136–138.

30. Sayers to Count Michael de la Bedoyere, editor of *The Catholic Herald*, October 7, 1941, *Letters*, 2:310.

31. James Welch to Sayers, June 1942, quoted *Letters*, 2:364; Sayers to Eric Fenn, July 14, 1940, *Letters*, 2:171.

32. Sayers, "Creed or Chaos?," 31.

33. Sayers, "Other Six Deadly Sins," 103.

34. Sayers, "Other Six Deadly Sins," 112.

35. See Max Weber, *The Protestant Ethic and the Spirit of Capitalism*, trans. Talcott Parsons (New York: Dover, 2003).

36. Sayers, "Creed or Chaos?," 51.

37. Krish Kandiah, "Church as Family," *Christianity Today* 63, no. 1 (Jan–Feb 2019): 69 (emphasis mine); LifeWay Research, "Parsing Prosperity," *Christianity Today* 62, no. 9 (November 2018): 16; LifeWay Research, "Our Favorite Heresies," *Christianity Today* 62, no. 10 (December 2018): 21.

38. Douthat, *Bad Religion*, 191 (emphasis mine).

39. Sayers, "Thought for the Day," in *Christ of the Creeds and Other Broadcast Messages to the British People during World War II*, ed. Suzanne Bray (West Sussex, GB: The Dorothy L. Sayers Society, 2008), 97.

40. Sayers, *Whose Body?* (New York: Avon, 1961), 118.

41. Carter Lindberg, *The European Reformations* (Oxford: Wiley-Blackwell, 2010), 59–60.

42. Sayers's statement appears in her notes to the fifth play. See *Man Born to Be King*, 124.

43. Sayers, *The Just Vengeance* (London: Gollancz, 1946), 56.

44. Sayers to Stephen Grenfell Esq., June 19, 1943, in *Christ of the Creeds*, 81.

45. Sayers, *Man Born to Be King*, 105.

46. Sayers, *Man Born to Be King*, 106.

47. Sayers, *Man Born to Be King*, 301.

48. Sayers, *Man Born to Be King*, 301.

49. Sayers, *Man Born to Be King*, 44, 46.

50. Sayers, *Man Born to Be King*, 306.

51. Sayers, *Man Born to Be King*, 281, 41.

52. Sayers, *Man Born to Be King*, 88.

53. Sayers, *Man Born to Be King*, 69 (emphasis mine).

54. Sayers, *Man Born to Be King*, 70 (emphasis mine).

55. Sayers, "Creed or Chaos?," 49.

56. Sayers, "Christ of the Creeds," 42.

57. Sayers, "Touchstone of History," in *Christ of the Creeds and Other Broadcast Messages to the British People during World War II*, ed.

Suzanne Bray (West Sussex, GB: The Dorothy L. Sayers Society, 2008), 69.

58. Sayers, "Touchstone," 69.

59. Sayers, *Man Born to Be King*, 218. (See Matthew 19, Mark 10, Luke 18.)

60. Sayers to Kathleen M. Penn, May 15, 1942, *Letters*, 2:361.

61. Sayers to James Welch, November 20, 1943, in *Christ of the Creeds*, 93.

62. Sayers, "Triumph of Easter," 13.

63. Sayers to H. S. Vere-Hodge, December 12, 1956, *Letters*, 4:353.

64. Sayers, *Man Born to Be King*, 214.

65. Sayers, *Man Born to Be King*, 214

66. C. S. Lewis, *The Great Divorce* (New York: Macmillan, 1970), 72.

67. Sayers to Maurice Brown, November 22, 1946, *Letters*, 3:276.

68. Sayers, *Mind of the Maker*, 135, 136, 137.

69. Sayers to Barbara Reynolds, March 28, 1956, *Letters*, 4:274.

70. C. S. Lewis, *The Last Battle* (New York: Collier, 1970), 164–65.

71. Sayers to John Cournos, December 4, 1924; October 27, 1924; *Letters*, 1:222, 218.

72. Sayers to Cournos, August 13, 1925, *Letters*, 1:237.

73. Sayers to Cournos, February 22, 1925, *Letters*, 1:230.

74. Marion Baker Fairman, "The Neo-Medieval Plays of Dorothy L. Sayers" (PhD dissertation, University of Pittsburgh, 1961), 91–92.

75. Sayers, *Zeal of Thy House*, 17.

76. Sayers, *Zeal of Thy House*, 25, 60 (emphasis mine).

77. Sayers, *Zeal of Thy House*, 74, 76.

78. Sayers, *Zeal of Thy House*, 76.

79. Sayers, "Other Six Deadly Sins," 85, 86.

80. Sayers, "Other Six Deadly Sins," 86.

81. Sayers to George S. Purkis, January 27, 1949, *Letters*, 3:424.

Chapter 3

1. Sayers to Eric Whelpton, February 22, 1954, *Letters*, 4:132.

2. Sayers to Rev. Dom. R. Russell, October 28, 1941, *Letters*, 2:316.

3. Sayers, *Man Born to Be King*, 181; see also John 9:3.

4. Sayers, *Man Born to Be King*, 181.

5. Sayers, *Man Born to Be King*, 182.

6. Sayers, *Man Born to Be King*, 183.

7. Sayers, *Man Born to Be King*, 185.

8. Sayers, *Man Born to Be King*, 186 (emphasis mine).

9. Sayers, *Man Born to Be King*, 109.

10. Sayers, *Man Born to Be King*, 167.

11. Sayers, *Man Born to Be King*, 108.

12. Sayers to James Welch, July 23, 1940, *Letters*, 2:172.

13. Sayers, *Man Born to Be King*, 139 (emphasis mine).

14. Sayers, "Charles Williams: A Poet's Critic," in *The Poetry of Search and the Poetry of Statement* (Eugene, OR: Wipf and Stock Publishers, 1963), 79.

15. For theologians who discuss "handing over," and their relevance to Sayers, see Crystal Downing, *Writing Performances: The Stages of Dorothy L. Sayers* (New York: Palgrave, 2004), 122–23.

16. Sayers, *Man Born to Be King*, 186.

17. Sayers, "Meaning of Purgatory," 75.

18. Sayers, Introduction to *The Comedy of Dante Alighieri the Florentine, Cantica I: Inferno,* trans. Dorothy L. Sayers (London: Penguin, 1949), 11.

19. Sayers to Charles Williams, September 26, 1944, *Letters*, 3:82.

20. Sayers, Introduction to *The Comedy of Dante Alighieri the Florentine, Cantica II: Purgatory*, trans. Dorothy L. Sayers (London: Penguin, 1955), 58.

21. Sayers, "Meaning of Purgatory," 88.

22. Sayers, Introduction to *Inferno,* 54–55.

23. Sayers, "The Church's Responsibility," 57–58 (emphasis mine).

24. Henri de Lubac, SJ, *Corpus Mysticum: The Eucharist and the Church in the Middle Ages*, trans. Gemma Simmonds CJ, et al., ed. Laurence Paul Hemming and Susan Frank Parsons (Notre Dame, IN: University of Notre Dame Press, 2006), 258–59.

25. Charles Keown, "The Controversial Organ," Lakewood Baptist Church, published March 4, 2014, accessed August 30, 2019, https://tinyurl.com/rfhlr7c.

26. Sayers, "Dogma is the Drama," 22.

27. Leon Morris, "Atonement," in *A Dictionary of Biblical Tradition in English Literature*, ed. David Lyle Jeffrey (Grand Rapids, MI: Eerdmans, 1992), 62.

28. Sayers to Marjorie Barber, October 26, 1942, *Letters*, 2:380.

29. Sayers, *Man Born to Be King*, 336–37.

30. David Lyle Jeffrey and Martin E. Marty, "Heresy," in *A Dictionary of Biblical Tradition in English Literature*, 345–46.

31. Sayers, "Is there a Definite Evil Power that attacks People in the Same Way as there is a Good Power that influences People?," in *Asking them Questions: A Selection from the Three Series,* ed. Ronald Selby Wright (London: Oxford University Press, 1953), 47, 48.

32. Alister E. McGrath, *Historical Theology: An Introduction to the History of Christian Thought* (Malden, MA: Blackwell, 1998), 136.

33. Sayers to Father Herbert Kelly, October 19, 1937, *Letters*, 2:54.

34. Richard Viladesau, *The Beauty of the Cross: The Passion of Christ in Theology and the Arts—From the Catacombs to the Eve of the Renaissance* (New York: Oxford University Press, 2006), 71.

35. Sayers, Introduction to *Man Born to Be King*, 12 note 5.

36. Sayers to Rev. Dom. R. Russell, October 28, 1941, *Letters*, 2:316.

37. Sayers to Professor G. L. Bickersteth, June 12, 1957, *Letters*, 4:394.

38. Sayers, *Man Born to Be King*, 246.

39. Sayers, "My Belief about Heaven and Hell," *The Sunday Times*, January 6, 1957, 8.

40. Sayers, "Heaven and Hell," 8.

41. Sayers to C. S. Lewis, November 4, 1949, *Letters*, 3:464.

42. Sayers to Professor G. L. Bickersteth, June 12, 1957, *Letters*, 4:395.

43. Sayers to Rev. C. Lattey, September 21, 1945, *Letters*, 3:158.

44. Sayers to G. H. Hawkins, May 23, 1944, *Letters*, 3:12.

45. Philip Ball, "Quantum Leaps, Long Assumed to Be Instantaneous, Take Time," *Quanta Magazine*, published June 5, 2019, accessed July 9, 2019, https://tinyurl.com/yxhcq9av.

46. Sayers, *Man Born to Be King*, 222.

47. Sayers, "Dogma Is the Drama," 23.

48. The chemist was Kenneth Hutton and the book was published by Penguin. See editor's note on page 158 of Sayers *Letters*, vol. 4.

49. Sayers, "Triumph of Easter," 15.

50. L. T. Duff to Sayers, March 15, 1943, in Sayers *Letters*, 2:391. Duff had listened to a re-broadcast in 1943.

51. Sayers to L. T. Duff, March 22, 1943, *Letters*, 2:392.

52. L. T. Duff to Sayers, March 30, 1943, *Letters*, 2:396.

53. Sayers to L. T. Duff, May 10, 1943, *Letters*, 2:401.

54. Robert Wright, *The Moral Animal: Evolutionary Psychology and Everyday Life* (New York: Vintage, 1994), 383.

55. Sayers to L. T. Duff, June 9, 1944, *Letters*, 3:18 (emphasis hers).

56. Sayers to L. T. Duff, June 9, 1944, *Letters*, 3:19.

57. Sayers to James Welch, February 19, 1942, *Letters*, 2:352.

58. Sayers to James Welch, February 19, 1942, *Letters*, 2:351.

59. Sayers to James Welch, February 19, 1942, *Letters*, 2:352.

60. Sayers to Count Michael de la Bedoyere, October 7, 1941, *Letters*, 2:309.

61. For Lewis on the Ecumenical Councils, see Suzanne Bray, "C. S. Lewis as an Anglican," 19–36.

62. Sayers to Count Michael de la Bedoyere, October 7, 1941, *Letters*, 2:309.

63. Sayers to John Wren-Lewis, June 18, 1954, *Letters*, 4:166.

64. Sayers to Barbara Reynolds, August 17, 1957, *Letters*, 4:410 (emphasis hers).

65. Sayers, "Church's Responsibility," 78.

Chapter 4

1. Sayers, "The Omnibus of Crime (1928–29)," in *The Art of the Mystery Story: A Collection of Critical Essays*, ed. Howard Haycraft (New York: Biblo & Tannen, 1976), 108.

2. Sayers, *Zeal of Thy House*, 103.

3. Robert E. Stone, "I Am Who I Am," in *Eerdmans Dictionary of the Bible,* ed. David Noel Freedman, Allen C. Myers, and Astrid B. Beck (Grand Rapids, MI: Eerdmans, 2000), 624.

4. Sayers, *Zeal of Thy House*, 103.

5. Sayers to Father Herbert Kelly, October 4, 1937, *Letters*, 2:45 (emphasis hers).

6. Sayers clarifies this distinction in a letter to Mrs. Robert Darby, April 7, 1948, *Letters*, 3:362.

7. Sayers to John Wren-Lewis, Good Friday, March 1954, *Letters*, 4:139.

8. G. K. Chesterton, *Orthodoxy*, ed. Craig M. Kibler (Lenoir, NC: Reformation Press, 2002), 37.

9. Sayers to Rev. C. Lattey, September 21, 1945, *Letters*, 3:158.

10. Sayers to Mrs. G. K. Chesterton, June 15, 1936, *Letters*, 1:394.

11. Sayers to her parents, February 1909, *Letters*, 1:18. In 1949, Sayers tells a correspondent that she "devoured" Chesterton's *Orthodoxy* at age fifteen, which means she read the book not long after her parents recommended it. See Sayers to Joan Nolan, October 12, 1949, *Letters*, 3:462.

12. Sayers to E. C. Bentley, July 20, 1937, *Letters*, 2:33.

13. C. S. Lewis, Introduction to *Phantastes and Lilith*, by George MacDonald (Grand Rapids, MI: Eerdmans, 1964), 11.

14. Lewis, Introduction to *Phantastes*, 12.

15. Sayers to Barbara Reynolds, February 10, 1956, *Letters*, 4:271.

16. Sayers to Barbara Reynolds, December 21, 1955, *Letters*, 4:264.

17. Sayers to G. L. A. Spafford, March 20, 1947, *Letters*, 3:300, 302 (emphasis mine).

18. J. R. R. Tolkien, "On Fairy-Stories," in *Essays Presented to Charles Williams*, ed. C. S. Lewis (Grand Rapids, MI: Eerdmans, 1966), 67.

19. C. S. Lewis, "It All Began with a Picture . . . ," in *On Stories, and Other Essays on Literature*, ed. Walter Hooper (New York: Harvest, 1982), 53.

20. See Roger Lancelyn Green and Walter Hooper, *C. S. Lewis: A Biography* (New York: Harcourt, Brace, Jovanovich, 1974), 249.

21. Sayers to Brother George Every, July 10, 1947, *Letters*, 3:314, 315.

22. Sayers to C. S. Lewis, December 12, 1955, *Letters*, 4:261.

23. Sayers to Rev. Aubrey Moody, October 18, 1954, *Letters*, 4:171.

24. Sayers to Lady Lees, August 29, 1944, *Letters*, 3:63–64.

25. Sayers to C. S. Lewis, July 31, 1946, *Letters*, 3:253.

26. C. S. Lewis to Sayers, July 23, 1946, *CSL Letters*, 2:721.

27. C. S. Lewis to Sayers, July 29, 1946, *CSL Letters*, 2:728.

28. Sayers to C. S. Lewis, July 31, 1946, *Letters*, 3:252.

29. Sayers to C. S. Lewis, July 31, 1946, *Letters*, 3:254.

30. Sayers to Lady Lees, August 29, 1944, *Letters*, 3:64.

31. Sayers, "Why Work?," 79–80.

32. Sayers didn't realize that the Hebrew word for "good" implies effective function. Nevertheless, functionality doesn't necessarily imply utility.

33. Sayers, *Man Born to Be King*, 185.

34. Sayers, *Zeal of Thy House*, 68.

35. Sayers, *Zeal of Thy House*, 99.

36. Sayers, "Greatest Drama Ever Staged," 4.

37. Sayers, *Mind of the Maker*, 122.

38. Sayers to Rev. F. W. Rowlands, February 22, 1946, *Letters*, 3:201.

39. Sayers to Rev. F. W. Rowlands, February 22, 1946, *Letters*, 3:201.

40. Sayers to C. S. Lewis, December 12, 1955, *Letters*, 4:261.

41. Sayers to C. S. Lewis, December 12, 1955, *Letters*, 4:260.

42. Sayers to the editor of *The BBC Quarterly*, January 27, 1947, *Letters*, 3:291.

43. Sayers, *Mind of the Maker*, 173.

44. Sayers, *Mind of the Maker*, 173.

45. Sayers, *Mind of the Maker*, 177.

46. Sayers, "Why Work?," 78.

47. Sayers to G. H. Hawkins, May 23, 1944, *Letters*, 3:12.

48. Sayers, *Mind of the Maker*, 121.

49. Sayers, "Why Work?," 73.

50. Sayers, "Why Work?," 68.

51. Sayers, "Why Work?," 66.

52. Sayers, "Other Six Deadly Sins," 99.

53. Sayers, *Man Born to Be King*, 218.

54. Sayers, "Why Work?," 63.

55. Sayers to R. Stephen Talmage, April 12, 1954, *Letters*, 4:154.

56. Sayers, *Mind of the Maker*, 215.

57. Sayers to the editor of the *Guardian*, January 15, 1939, *Letters*, 2:112.

58. Sayers, *Man Born to Be King*, 264, 173.

59. Sayers, *Mind of the Maker*, 27.

60. Crystal Downing, *Changing Signs of Truth: A Christian Introduction to the Semiotics of Communication* (Downer's Grove, IL: IVP Academic, 2012), 322.

61. Sayers, Introduction to *Man Born to Be King*, 3.

62. Sayers to R. S. Pratt, January 19, 1956, *Letters*, 4:269.

63. Sayers, "Greatest Drama Ever Staged," 7.

64. Sayers, "Dogma Is the Drama," 24.

65. Sayers to the Rev. Dom. R. Russell, October 28, 1941, *Letters*, 2:315.

66. Sayers, "Are Women Human?," in *Are Women Human?* (Grand Rapids: Eerdmans, 1971), 28–29.

67. Sayers to C. S. Lewis, July 31, 1946, *Letters*, 3:253.

68. Sayers to C. S. Lewis, July 31, 1946, *Letters*, 3:253.

69. Sayers to Barbara Reynolds, November 5, 1956, *Letters*, 4:343–44.

70. Sayers, *Mind of the Maker*, 122.

71. Sayers to Professor G. L. Bickersteth, June 20, 1955, *Letters*, 4:241.

72. Sayers to John Wren-Lewis, Good Friday, March 1954, *Letters*, 4:140; Sayers to unknown correspondent, November 28, 1941, *Letters*, 2:329.

Chapter 5

1. Sayers, "Greatest Drama Ever Staged," 5 (emphasis hers).

2. F. M. L. Thompson, "William Joynson-Hicks, 1st Viscount Brentford," *Dictionary of National Biography*, ed. Colin Matthew (Oxford: Oxford University Press, 2004), 39.

3. Sayers, "Greatest Drama Ever Staged," 5.

4. Sayers to Derek McCulloch, November 5, 1940, *Letters*, 2:190 (emphasis mine).

5. Sayers, Introduction to *Man Born to Be King*, 7.

6. Sayers to Rev. Eric Fenn, March 20, 1941, *Letters*, 2:242.

7. Sayers, *Man Born to Be King*, 102.

8. Sayers, Introduction to *Man Born to Be King*, 14.

9. Sayers, *Man Born to Be King*, 132.

10. Sayers, *Man Born to Be King,* 132–33.

11. Sayers, *Man Born to Be King*, 102 (emphasis mine).

12. Barbara Reynolds, *Dorothy L. Sayers: Her Life and Soul* (New York: St. Martin's, 1993), 296.

13. Sayers, *Man Born to Be King*, 125.

14. Sayers to J. D. Upcott, September 1, 1941, *Letters*, 2:291.

15. Sayers, *Man Born to Be King*, 103.

16. Sayers, *Man Born to Be King*, 151.

17. Sayers, *Man Born to Be King*, 164.

18. Sayers, *Man Born to Be King,* 194.

19. Sayers, Introduction to *Man Born to Be King,* 7.

20. Sayers, *Man Born to Be King*, 257–58.

21. Sayers to Barbara Reynolds, August 17, 1957, *Letters*, 4:410.

22. Mark A. Noll, *The Civil War as a Theological Crisis* (Chapel Hill, NC: University of North Carolina Press, 2006), 115, 49 (emphasis mine).

23. Mark Galli, "Where We Got It Wrong," *Christianity Today*, 62 (December 2018): 28.

24. Sayers, "Is there a Definite Evil Power," 49, 51.

25. Sayers to Dr. J. H. Oldham, September 10, 1939, *Letters*, 2:133.

26. Sayers, "The Church in the New Age," *World Review*, March 1941, 12.

27. Sayers, "Church in the New Age," 12.

28. Sayers to Barbara Reynolds, February 21, 1950, *Letters*, 3:491.

29. Sayers to Joyce Reason, February 23, 1950, *Letters*, 3:492.

30. Sayers to Dr. W. W. Greg, October 18, 1940, *Letters*, 2:184.

31. Sayers, "Helen Simpson," *The Fortnightly*, January 1941, 58.

32. Sayers, *Zeal of Thy House*, 46.

33. Sayers, "Why Work?," 78.

34. Sayers, *Mind of the Maker*, 223.

35. Sayers to L. T. Duff, June 9, 1944, *Letters*, 3:18.

36. Sayers, *Mind of the Maker*, 205, 206, 209 (emphasis hers).

37. Sayers, *Man Born to Be King*, 54.

38. Sayers, *Man Born to Be King*, 57.

39. Sayers, *Man Born to Be King*, 59.

40. Sayers, *Murder Must Advertise*, 356 (emphasis mine).

41. Sayers, "Other Six Deadly Sins," 112.

42. Sayers, *Man Born to Be King*, 163.

43. Sayers, "Church in the New Age," 12.

44. Sayers to Sir Richard Acland, April 17, 1940, *Letters*, 2:160, 161.

45. Sayers to John Anthony Fleming, June 30, 1945, *Letters*, 3:152.

46. Unpublished letter from Sayers to Tom Driberg, Esq., June 8, 1945, archived at the Marion E. Wade Center in Wheaton, IL. See Sayers Papers, Wade File 111, p. 8.

47. Sayers, "You Are the Treasury," Sayers Papers, Wade File 147.

48. Sayers, "Creed or Chaos?," and "Other Six Deadly Sins," 52, 97.

49. Sayers to J. D. Upcott, September 1, 1941, *Letters*, 2:291–92.

50. Sayers, *The Emperor Constantine*, 143.

51. Sayers, "Six Other Deadly Sins," 110, 111.

52. Sayers, *Just Vengeance,* 314.

53. Sayers, *Just Vengeance*, 288, 340.

54. Sayers, "Church in the New Age," 14 (emphasis mine).

55. Sayers, "Target Area," in *Poetry of Dorothy L. Sayers*, ed. Ralph E. Hone (Cambridge: Dorothy L. Sayers Society, 1996), lines 133–34.

56. Sayers, Introduction to *Man Born to Be King,* 5.

57. David Lyle Jeffrey and Martin E. Marty, "Heresy," in *A Dictionary of Biblical Tradition in English Literature*, ed. David Lyle Jeffrey (Grand Rapids, MI: Eerdmans, 1992), 345.

58. Sayers to Maurice Browne, October 28, 1946, *Letters*, 3:275.

59. Sayers to Dr. J. H. Oldham, October 2, 1939, *Letters*, 2:137.

60. "A Statement of Aims for the proposed Bridgehead series of books," Appendix to James Brabazon, *Dorothy L. Sayers: A Biography* (New York: Scribner's, 1981), 278–82.

61. Sayers, *Mind of the Maker*, 111.

62. Sayers, *Mind of the Maker*, 177.

63. Sayers, *Begin Here: A Wartime Essay* (London: Gollancz, 1942), 19.

64. Sayers, *Mind of the Maker*, 214, 137 (emphasis mine).

65. Noll, *Civil War as a Theological Crisis*, 42.

66. Sayers, *Mind of the Maker*, 187.

67. Sayers, *Mind of the Maker*, 215.

68. Sayers to A. C. Capey, April 14, 1954, *Letters*, 4:154.
69. Sayers to Father Taylor, sometime after March 8, 1942, *Letters*, 2:355.
70. Sayers to James Welch, July 25, 1946, *Letters*, 3:249.
71. For a helpful overview of Sayers's emphasis on community throughout her life, see Christine A. Colón, *Choosing Community: Action, Faith, and Joy in the Works of Dorothy L. Sayers* (Downer's Grove, IL: InterVarsity, 2019).
72. Nott, *The Emperor's Clothes*, 31.
73. Sayers to Barbara Reynolds, January 5, 1955, *Letters*, 4:205.
74. Sayers, "A Debate Deferred: The Dogma in the Manger," *VII: An Anglo-American Literary Review* 3 (1982), 44 (emphasis hers).
75. Sayers, *Just Vengeance*, 327.
76. Genesis 4:1–15. The translation by Hebrew specialist Robert Alter demonstrates God's avoidance of exchangism: "And the Lord said to Cain, 'Why are you incensed, and why is your face fallen? For *whether you offer well, or whether you do not*, at the tent flap sin crouches and for you is its longing, but you will rule over it'" (vv. 6–7, emphasis mine). It's all about the consequences of human choice. See Robert Alter, *The Five Books of Moses: A Translation with Commentary* (New York: Norton, 2008).
77. Sayers to Canon Linwood Wright, March 21, 1946, *Letters*, 3:212.
78. Sayers to J. Wilshin, August 21, 1941, *Letters*, 2:286.

Chapter 6

1. Sayers, *Mind of the Maker*, 208–9.
2. Sayers, "The Church's Responsibility," 57–58 (emphasis mine).
3. Sayers to Albert Hodgson, September 12, 1951, *Letters*, 4:21–22.
4. Sayers to Barbara Reynolds, September 5, 1956, *Letters*, 4:327.

INDEX

advertising, 51-53, 155, 192
Anglicanism, 22, 62, 63
Anselm of Canterbury, 110-11
Are Women Human? 8-9, 164
Arius, 36-38, 44-45, 152, 119, 198
art for art's sake, 151
Athanasius, 119
atheism, 42, 58, 60, 61
atonement, 107-14, 117, 118, 124-25, 213

baptism, 99
Beatles, the, 105
Bebbington, David, 63-64
belief, 24, 35, 43, 56, 64, 69, 71-73, 77, 84, 91, 97-99, 109, 121-22, 139, 163, 195, 199, 212-13
Bible and/or Biblicism, 10, 26, 29-33, 35-38, 45, 49, 63-65, 69-70, 78, 81-82, 92, 97-98, 101-02, 107, 121, 137, 157, 182-83, 198, 206

born again, 14, 80, 160-62, 165, 169
both/and paradigms, 43-45, 47-49, 105, 117, 118, 122-23, 138, 148, 189, 195-96, 198-99, 200, 204-209, 212-13
Bridgeheads, 202
British Broadcasting Corporation (BBC), 17, 25-32, 55, 58-59, 66, 69, 70, 77, 79-80, 96, 123-24, 126, 151, 156, 172, 180
Brown, Janice, 38

Cain and Abel, 198, 200, 201, 205, 206, 208, 209
Calvin, John, 63
Calvinism, 80-81
capitalism, 89, 155, 157, 195, 197, 199, 204
Catholic Herald, The, 66, 126
certitude, 96-98, 115-17, 177, 182, 189, 191-92, 196-98

Chesterton, G. K., 1, 18, 136-39, 141, 143; *Napoleon of Notting Hill, The,* 138, 143; *Orthodoxy,* 137, 138, 143, 228n11

Christendom: A Journal of Christian Sociology, 8-9

Christianity Today, 68, 183

Christie, Agatha, 18-19

Churchill, Winston, 27, 31

"Church in the New Age, The", 185, 199

communication and rhetoric, 8, 12, 17, 24-25, 29-30, 33, 43, 140-41, 156-70, 189, 203-07, 213

consumerism, 51-53, 149, 153, 155, 165, 192

conversion, 5, 20, 32, 64, 65, 72

Cournos, John, 85

creativity (see chapter four)

"Creed or Chaos", 197

Creeds, the, 35, 37-39, 41, 43-44, 47-48, 64, 66, 70, 91-92, 99, 107, 115, 117, 118, 121, 122-23, 126, 173, 213; see also Nicene Creed

Crucifixion, the, 3, 10, 12, 15, 25, 26, 60, 64, 71, 76, 109, 193

Dante Alighieri and/or *The Divine Comedy,* 13, 35, 81, 103-4, 116

demythologizers, 10

Derrida, Jacques, 55

Detection Club, The, 18

Documents in the Case, The, 120

dogma / doctrine, 11, 14, 15, 28, 35-38, 40-49, 56-61, 65-66, 70, 76-77, 83, 88-89, 91, 107, 109, 117, 121, 122, 125-28, 134, 152, 168, 173, 177

dogmatism, 40, 42, 56

Douthat, Ross, 68-69

Duff, L. T., 121-22

Ecumenical Councils, 35-36, 38-40, 43, 46, 49, 71, 91, 107, 114, 118, 125-26, 128, 206

Eliot, T.S., 20, 209

Emperor Constantine, The, 36, 38, 44, 119, 198

Eucharist, 28, 62, 63, 80, 100, 101

Evangelicalism, 2, 3, 63-68, 72, 137, 169, 183

evangelism, 23-25, 64-66, 142-47, 165

exchangism / economy of exchange, 54-55, 61, 63, 65, 67-78, 81-82, 84-88, 90, 92-95, 97, 99, 102-06, 108-09, 111, 112, 117, 123, 144, 147, 148, 150, 151, 154-55, 157-59, 163, 189-93, 195, 208

Fleming, Atherton (Mac), 22, 23, 85, 134, 165

Fleming, John Anthony, 85-86

forgiveness, 29, 81, 88, 125
free will and/or determinism, 43,
    59-60, 80-84, 103-4

Galileo, 50, 220n56
"Gargoyle, The", 3
Gaudy Night, 19-21
gender, 7-9, 20, 140, 164,
    204-05
gift of love, 54, 60, 71, 76-77, 79,
    81-82, 87-88, 90, 91, 93-94,
    102, 112, 117, 127, 189,
    207-08
"Greatest Drama Ever Staged,
    The", 24

Health and Wealth Gospel,
    68-69
Heaven and/or Hell, 80-81, 82,
    103, 115-17, 162, 198
heresy, 36, 39, 40-42, 43-47,
    56, 110, 127-28, 152, 195,
    198, 201, 212; Arian, 36-38,
    44-45, 47, 152, 198; Docetic,
    45-47; Gnostic, 201, 203;
    Manichaean, 110, 152
Hitler, Adolph, 15, 23, 57-60,
    176-77, 180-1, 196, 199
Holocaust, the, 58-60
Holy Spirit, 30, 37, 65, 69, 83,
    98, 126, 128, 133, 143, 152,
    173
Hughes, Robert, 17-18

idolatry, 33, 43, 145, 162, 170,
    176

imago Dei, 132-35, 142, 143, 146,
    148-49, 153-58, 160, 167-68,
    203-05, 211-13
Incarnation, 12, 35, 47-49, 62,
    107, 114-15, 128, 169, 200-
    01, 205, 211-12

Indulgences, 70, 102-03, 111-12
integrity of work, 21-23, 27, 40,
    41, 146, 187-89, 190, 196

Jesus as subversive, 5, 9, 24, 25,
    48-50, 71, 100-01, 113, 159-
    60, 163, 171-71, 174-75, 183,
    212
Jones, A. H. M., 174, 175-76
Josephus, 74
Joynson-Hicks, William, 171
judgment as consequences, 47,
    77-81, 84-88, 189, 193-94,
    196
Just Vengeance, The, 34, 70-71,
    198-99, 208

Keown, Charles, 106

Lewis, C. S., 1-2, 32, 35, 42, 50,
    63, 64, 82-84, 103, 125-26,
    139-45, 150, 157, 163, 165,
    209;
logical positivism, 136-37, 139-41
Lubac, Henri de, 105
Luther, Martin, 39, 49, 70, 102

MacDonald, George, 139, 141
Machiavelli, Niccolo, 194

Man Born to Be King, The, 17,
25-34, 55, 70, 72-76, 79, 82,
91-97, 99-100, 108-09, 112,
113, 115, 117-18, 119-21, 123,
145-47, 152, 156, 159-60,
172-82, 185, 188-89, 191-
92, 194, 200, 204, 205, 212;
Barabbas in, 181; Baruch in,
97, 174-76, 178, 181-82, 188,
191-92, 196; Caiaphas in,
95, 160, 178-82, 188, 191,
196; controversy over, 27-32,
55, 79, 91, 99, 100, 117-18,
123-24, 204 ; Crucifixion in,
73, 75, 76; disciples in, 26,
29, 72-73, 76, 92-93, 95, 99,
108-09, 115; Gethsemane in,
95, 115; Herod in, 74-76, 96,
172; John the Baptist in, 191-
92; Judas in, 95-97, 99-100,
107, 113, 117, 119-20, 160,
174-75, 177, 191-92, 196;
Magi in, 74-75, 172; man
born blind in, 92-94, 107,
113, 116, 147, 212; Nicodemus in, 159-60, 180 ; Pharisees in, 94, 97, 174, 177-78;
Sanhedrim in, 178-80, 182,
194 ; Triumphal Entry in,
96-97, 175 ; Zealots in, 96,
97, 174-75, 182, 191
Marcion, 49
Maritain, Jacques, 188
McGrath, Alister, 111
mercy and/or justice, 53-54,
81-82, 84, 87, 199, 208

Mind of the Maker, The, 83-84,
134-36, 149, 152-53, 156,
158, 160-61, 169, 189, 190,
201-204, 211
"Mocking of Christ, The", 3-4,
6-7, 14
Munt, Sally, 20
Murder Must Advertise, 52, 192

Nazism, 57-59, 176-77, 180, 182,
199, 201
Nicene Creed, the, 35-36, 41, 91,
99, 107, 115, 118, 126, 198,
213,
Noll, Mark, 182-83
Nott, Kathleen, 42-43, 207-09

Origen, 104-05
"Other Six Deadly Sins, The", 53,
88-89, 155, 193, 197, 198

piety, 5, 13, 117, 137, 161
politics, 3, 5, 6, 7, 24, 38, 43, 57,
75, 89, 95, 96-97, 126-28,
151, 161, 170-209 ; conservative and/or liberal, 127, 173-
77, 180-83, 185-89, 196-97,
206 ; Labour Party, 186, 189,
197 ; Nationalism, 176, 179-
81 ; Polarization in, 169-70,
173, 177, 95, 205 ; religion
and, 3, 6, 24, 38, 39, 43, 57,
89, 128, 161, 177-82, 206
predestination, 80-81
prosperity theology (see Health
and Wealth Gospel)

Purgatory, 98, 102-04

quietism, 186, 189
Quintilian, 164

racism, 57-60, 180, 183-84, 199
relativism, 55-59, 61, 83
resurrection, Christ's, 15, 71, 107-09, 117, 192
Reynolds, Barbara, 28, 34, 176, 213
Rorty, Richard, 56

"Sacrament of Matter, The", 46
Sacraments / Sacramentalism, 61-64
salvation / redemption, 6, 32, 61, 62, 64, 70-72, 76-77, 80-81, 84-85, 87-88 , 92, 94, 102, 106-07, 112-13, 192, 195, 199, 200, 208
sanctification, 20, 195
Santa Claus / Father Christmas, 71
Satan/devil, 109-11, 184
Sayers, Dorothy Leigh, biography (published works listed separately)
as advertising copywriter, 8, 51, 85, 192; as Canterbury playwright, 20-23, 25, 27, 47-48, 63, 86-87, 110; childhood / adolescence, 2, 62, 105, 136, 138; Church confirmation, 62-63; as Dante translator, 13, 103-4, 220n56;

death, 1, 51, 90; as detective novelist, 18-22, 25, 51-52, 54, 69, 89, 131, 137; marriage, 2-3, 22, 23, 85, 134, 165; as mother, 3, 85-86; as Oxford University student, 2, 7, 8, 105, 137; parents, 2, 4, 61-62, 85, 138; "personal angle" defiance, 18, 41, 91-92; as poet, 3-4, 6-7, 15, 20-21, 199; as politically engaged, 176, 186-87, 202; as school teacher, 7, 144
science, 42, 43, 58, 118-23, 137, 140, 141; quantum leaps, 118-20, 123
self-righteousness, 42, 86-87, 171
Shakespeare, William, 28, 48, 149, 154
Simpson, Helen, 187, 193, 202
sin, 15, 47, 64, 71, 76-77, 84, 85, 87-89, 94, 148, 168, 184, 198-99, 207
slavery and abolition, 126, 182-83, 204
Society of St. Anne, 13, 208-09
status quo, 4-10, 12, 13, 20, 29-30, 34, 48, 150, 159, 160, 183, 188, 189
Stowe, Harriet Beecher, 204-05
Strong Poison, 120

Tertullian, 156-57
"Thought for the Day", 68
Tolkien, J.R.R., 141-42, 143, 150-51, 157

Transubstantiation, 28, 101

Tribulation, the, 206

Trinity, the, 6, 36-37, 83, 128-29, 132-35, 149, 152, 156-57, 167, 203

Tyndale, William, 32, 39, 49, 106, 124-25

Unpopular Opinions, 8

Vane, Harriet, 19-20, 21, 54

Victoria, Queen of England, 8

Viladesau, Richard, 111

Weber, Max, 67

Welch, James, 28-31, 66, 70, 96, 124

Wells, H. G., 140-41

Whose Body?, 19, 69

"Why Work?", 156

Williams, Charles, 103, 104

Wimsey, Lord Peter, 18-19, 21, 22, 54, 69, 137

World War I, 1, 7, 57, 86

World War II, 26, 30, 31, 34, 57, 67, 123, 173, 176, 180, 197, 198, 202

Wright, Robert, 122

Wycliffe, John, 98-99, 124-25

Zeal of Thy House, The, 20-23, 40, 46, 47, 63, 86-88, 120, 132-34, 138-39, 146-48, 171, 185, 187-88